# Capoeira Beyond Brazil

# CAPOEIRA
## Beyond Brazil

From a Slave Tradition
to an International Way of Life

## Aniefre Essien

**BLUE SNAKE BOOKS**
*Berkeley, California*

Published by Blue Snake Books

Blue Snake Books' publications are distributed by
North Atlantic Books
P.O. Box 12327
Berkeley, California 94712

Cover photo by Ben Battersby
Cover and book design by Brad Greene
Printed in the United States of America

*Capoeira Beyond Brazil: From a Slave Tradition to an International Way of Life* is sponsored by the Society for the Study of Native Arts and Sciences, a nonprofit educational corporation whose goals are to develop an educational and cross-cultural perspective linking various scientific, social, and artistic fields; to nurture a holistic view of arts, sciences, humanities, and healing; and to publish and distribute literature on the relationship of mind, body, and nature.

North Atlantic Books' publications are available through most bookstores. For further information, call 800-733-3000 or visit our websites at www.northatlanticbooks.com and www.bluesnakebooks.com.

Library of Congress Cataloging-in-Publication Data

Essien, Aniefre.
    Capoeira beyond Brazil : from a slave tradition to an international way of life / by Aniefre Essien.
        p. cm.
    Summary: "A survey of capoeira written by a non-Brazilian authority includes technical instruction, rich and critical history, an exploration of training programs for at-risk youth, and a sociocultural consideration of the effects internationalization has had on this form"—Provided by publisher.
    ISBN 978-1-58394-255-0
    1. Capoeira (Dance) 2. Capoeira (Dance)—History. I. Title.
    GV1796.C145E77 2008
    793.3'1981—dc22
                                                        2008026627
                                                        CIP

1 2 3 4 5 6 7 8 9 VERSA 14 13 12 11 10 09 08

*Dedicated to the loving memory of my mother,*
Tennie

⁓

# Table of Contents

# Acknowledgments

To my brother Michael: thank you for securing me on my path as a man and as a martial artist. You provided me with the tools that I needed to be a fully developed martial artist and not just a fighter. Thank you (and Maya) for supporting me as I developed into a capoeirista, and later a capoeira teacher. And to my brother Anthony, you have been a role model and friend for my entire life.

To *meu irmão*, *meu amigo*, and *meu mestre*, Mestre Ralil: you have freely shared your wisdom not only in capoeira, but life as well. You have taught me how to navigate the rough-and-tumble seas of being a professor and a mestre of capoeira, modeling these qualities not only in what you say, but in what you do. You have brought me along from stage to stage in capoeira, always pushing me to be better and giving me the knowledge required to do so. I am honored to say that I am your student, am grateful for the time we have spent together, and look forward to the many years to come.

To my capoeira "uncles," Mestres Papiba, Edinho, Terry, Themba, Boneco, Marcelo, and Nenel: thank you for opening your doors for me without parameters and allowing me access to your capoeira worlds. The time and experiences I've had with you are cherished parts of my development as a capoeirista.

To my students: I was forced to grow up in capoeira quickly, and I would like to thank all of you, past and present, for being amazing students. Because you trusted me, and honored me by allowing me to be your teacher, I have in turn been allowed to learn from our interactions, struggles, and journeys together.

To the Raízes do Brasil family: I am inspired every time I wear our shirt, knowing who else is wearing it. From Oakland to San Francisco, Santa Cruz, Los Angeles, Union City, Brooklyn, Madison, all the way down to Brasília, São Paulo, Piaui, Rio Grande do Norte, and Caracas, I am proud to be in league with you all.

And last, but not least, I would like to thank Anastasia McGhee and Elizabeth Kennedy for helping to move this project from stage to stage preparing the book for release. Your assistance is truly appreciated.

—Aniefre Essien
Oakland, California, 2008

# Foreword

There are many books about capoeira, but this one certainly stands out by showing the reality in the world of capoeira. Aniefre—I know him as Tartaruga (Turtle)—explains both the practical and theoretical approaches to capoeira, together with the importance of these concepts in the life of capoeiristas, from the origins of the art to its modern expression (both admirable and not).

I respect Tartaruga as a capoeirista for his balance, involvement, and commitment. Even though he has had to face many difficulties, his achievements are rightfully recognized in the capoeira community, and he has brought a lot to the art of capoeira. Among these achievements were *batizados* (ceremonial contests/performances for belt or "cord" graduation); performances in schools, clubs, and theaters; a capoeira CD release; and the hosting of two capoeira tournaments with many capoeiristas in attendance from California and New York. He's been to Brazil several times, showing his technical proficiency and knowledge in *rodas* (circles or playing rings) with high-level Brazilian athletes. He opened an academy in Oakland, California, where he spent three years developing social projects with and for the city's needy.

I admire Tartaruga as a straightforward human being—for his character, for being a respectful son and present brother, an admired uncle, a supportive friend in tough moments, an exemplary teacher, and a dedicated student. Congratulations, Tartaruga, you are a model of life. God bless you.

Your friend, brother, and *mestre*,
Ralil Salomão

**Pickup Name:** MEN'S LACROSSE – COOK, T-ANNER

**BOX#:** 1813-1

W20

S

SA-COOK

**Customer Name:** SA-COOK, TANNER

**Order#:** 106022298-1

**Pickup Location:** AT STORE

PCK

**TO REORDER YOUR UPS DIRECT THERMAL LABELS:**

1. Access our supply ordering web site at **UPS.COM®**
   or Contact UPS at 800-877-8652.

2. Please refer to Label # 01774006 when ordering.

01774006    KR

# Introduction

It all began with a simple request: "Nef, come check out this capoeira class."

"What's capoeira?" I responded without interest.

My friend J.R. continued, "It's this martial ... something, something, something ... created by African slaves in Brazil."

That was all I needed to hear. I had practiced martial arts since I was a teenager, and to learn that there was a martial art created by black folks was twice as enticing. I always enjoyed seeing and learning about as many martial arts as possible. The Shaolin Kung Fu school that I was part of was far from dogmatic and encouraged us to appreciate other martial arts.

So eventually I went to visit the highly touted capoeira class on a Tuesday, along with my brother Michael, who actually had been my only martial arts instructor up to that point. We went just to watch. My brother was so moved that he returned to the class that Saturday to participate. I found the class interesting but didn't decide to actually take up capoeira right away. Because of my hectic school schedule (I was studying business at San Francisco State University), my part-time job, and my having already planned to add an additional Shaolin class on Saturdays down at the Shaolin temple, there really wasn't too much room for capoeira.

My brother returned home from capoeira class that Saturday afternoon, aching and complaining of having used muscles he never knew existed, yet absolutely pumped about what he experienced. My curiosity was aroused. Coincidentally, the instructor at the Shaolin temple whose class I had planned to attend cancelled his Saturday time slot, so I now had a free opening to train. Not knowing that my life was going to be changed forever, I accompanied my brother to capoeira class the following Saturday. The rest has been a heart-pumping blur of joy, pain, growth, learning, failing, learning more, forgetting a little, re-learning, stumbling, falling but never falling flat, doing *rolê* and returning to *ginga*, and all in all having a great time that has taught me one thing: I don't know anything.

Capoeira is far from a rigid art form and has constantly had to change throughout its history to adapt to the environment in which it exists. Consequently there are many different viewpoints (and books written) about what capoeira is, how it originated, who capoeira belongs to, and even how the instruments should be arranged in the *roda*.

The goal of this book is two-fold: to provide a contextual understanding of capoeira, and to share my unique viewpoint as a non-Brazilian capoeira instructor, who is also black.

Capoeira in its purest form is a celebration, and simultaneously a fight. The celebration is that of life and freedom from various forms of oppression, from slave masters, police, fears, insecurities, and a lack of coordination or confidence. The fight, which used to occur on plantations during slave rebellions, nowadays takes place inside the individual practitioner who's trying to understand who he or she is, and how to express that understanding of self with fluidity, control, and balance. Capoeira frequently, and unfortunately, becomes a fight between fellow capoeiristas, which makes the fight within that much more difficult to win.

People frequently try to squeeze capoeira into a nice, short, and precise word or phrase. That is a futile goal. Capoeira is a dance, but much more than a dance. Capoeira is a martial art, but much more than a martial art. Capoeira is a tradition of African slaves, but much more than a static tradition. Capoeira is all those things, constantly morphing to emphasize one more than the others, but always containing all the elements, and a few more, to become this intoxicating rhythmic motion of tricks, shows of strength and flexibility, displays of balance and grace, ancestral traditions, and lethal attacks.

The popularity of capoeira has increased remarkably over the years from its grassroots beginnings. A once-underground movement of the oppressed spread to become widely accepted. Capoeira went from local pastime to national fad, eventually becoming much more—a tradition within Brazilian culture. What was once practiced only by those on the lowest rung of Brazilian society came to be one of the greatest pastimes of all Brazil. From the plantations, then to the *favelas* (slums), capoeira grew to engulf Brazil, then spilled beyond Brazil's borders to the United States, Canada, Europe, and even returned to Africa— the ancestral land of its creators. I find it absolutely amazing that an individual can now learn capoeira in the United States and actualize his or her potential within the art form without having to move to a distant land.

The brilliance that emanates from capoeira is special, but far from mystical. Capoeira, like anything in life, is what you make it. Now that capoeira has truly arrived here in the United States, on what path will it travel as it evolves? Because of the immense wealth of this country, gross commercialization has already crept into capoeira, influencing its development here. What will we, as Americans, make of capoeira? What will we do with it? I hope that we will prove to be more than mere consumers of capoeira.

I hope that we become capoeiristas through and through. I have all too often seen students of capoeira try to emulate anything Brazilian in the quest to be counted as a capoeirista and prove to be nothing more than another fad follower, soon swept away by some other "ethnic" cultural activity. I have also frequently encountered capoeira students here in the United States with little to no ambition to reach any real level of proficiency, particularly tragic when it's a student with potential. This type of student may believe that simply because he or she was born here and not in Brazil that he or she is less gifted when it comes to capoeira. I have heard my mestre say countless times that the secret of capoeira is this: train capoeira!

Capoeira's future in the United States is bright, and I believe that anyone who calls him- or herself a capoeirista will strive to be more than someone looking for the latest exotic workout. Capoeira fueled the souls of those held in the most horrific oppressive conditions. It energized their spirits to carry on, to overcome whatever obstacles they could. Capoeira nourished the existence of countless downtrodden spirits, helping to lift them above their given situation in order to live on. After all their struggles, the world today is a better place. One of the fruits of their struggle is the fact that capoeira is still alive.

Another of the enduring legacies of capoeira is the sense of community that exists among capoeiristas. This community has grown, as stated before, from a micro-subset of Brazilian society to a global community containing members from countless backgrounds. The unifying thread is our love of capoeira and the way in which we *ginga* through life.

Wherever I travel I stumble upon capoeira, even when I am not looking for it. Wherever my students travel, I can send them to a great capoeira school. This is not just in Brazil, this is across the U.S., Canada, Japan, Italy, Spain, Venezuela, etc. Just within Raízes do Brasil, we have schools on several continents, including throughout the Americas and Europe. I am in fact a product of this internationalization of capoeira. The capoeira community has reached such a level of international development that I, as a non-Brazilian, have developed non-Brazilian students who are now teachers of capoeira.

With capoeira becoming more of a global community, inevitably there is the give and take of peoples from different parts of the world coming together and sharing space. Ideals that may be accepted by some may not be accepted by others. Customs that may be common only in some places may broaden and enhance the worldview of others.

With the culture of capoeira always evolving to adapt to each new generation, the new international nature of capoeira will inevitably affect the art form. How will the workout fad culture of the U.S. affect capoeira? How will the language barrier created by Japanese speakers affect the tradition of singing capoeira songs in Portuguese?

*Capoeira Beyond Brazil* looks at these types of questions, and tells stories from this new international capoeira community. New norms within capoeira are being established daily in Paris, Los Angeles, and Vancouver. While most of what has made up the folklore and tradition of capoeira is being perpetuated throughout the global capoeira community, traditions such as women not being respected as capoeiristas have been challenged and continue to be challenged.

There is an African tradition known as *Sankofa*. In short, *Sankofa* is signified by a bird flying forward while looking backward. The meaning of this symbol is that we should never forget our past, that we should look to it for understanding of who we are and build on the past experiences and wisdom of our ancestors as we move into the future. I hope that as capoeiristas we remain mindful of capoeira's past as we move forward into the *rodas* of tomorrow.

# 1

# Capoeira Origins

There are many disagreements regarding the origin of capoeira. Some say that it came from Africa, while others say that it originated in Brazil. There is validity to each stance, depending on how you define "originates." There is no doubt that capoeira proper developed in Brazil. Capoeira has spread all over the world, and it has been the masters of Brazil who have done this missionary work. On the other hand, no one denies that capoeira was created by African slaves based on African traditions. Additionally, the oral tradition of capoeira states that the practice comes from *N'golo*, a ritual from Angola. So is capoeira African, African-Brazilian, or Brazilian? This question ignites heated debate without fail.

Recorded history shows that capoeira is rooted in the *"Ma'afa"* or the "Great Tragedy" known also as the western slave trade. Africa was raped by the Portuguese, Dutch, Spanish, English, and other Europeans for her finest young men and women, who were forcibly taken west to live in slavery. The Portuguese colonized Brazil, and consequently this is where they took their African captives, primarily to the port cities of Salvador and Recife in the northeast, and to Rio de Janeiro in the south of Brazil. From here there are countless possibilities (and arguments) as to the next step in the development of capoeira.

One popular theory is that capoeira was created in the *senzalas,* or slave quarters, by Africans from different regions and cultures. It's believed that they combined aspects of each of their cultures to create a new art form—capoeira. The fundamental problem with this theory is the amount of time that it would take for this to have occurred. The earliest that you could have had slaves in Brazil from two different regions of Africa would have been in the early 1600s. From there, it would take time for this melding of cultures to occur, then even more time for this newly formed culture to spread. The northeast is considered to be the home of capoeira, but there are early records of capoeira in Rio de Janeiro in the south of Brazil as early as 1770.[1]

Others say that capoeira was created in the *quilombos,* or the sovereign communities established by escaped African slaves in the mountains and jungles of Brazil, as a means of self-defense from the Portuguese military. This explanation is interesting, to say the least, but not plausible. Capoeira in all likelihood existed in the *quilombos,* but to say that it originated there as a means of self-defense from Portuguese military forces doesn't hold water. The kicks, sweeps, and take-downs of capoeira are no match for cannons and bullets.

A third point of view is that capoeira was brought to Brazil from Africa, having developed from the African tradition known as *N'golo* or *Dança de Zebra.* This ritual mimics the fighting tactics of zebras and was played by young males as part of a puberty ritual. There's a *ladainha,* a type of song in Capoeira Angola, that describes capoeira as follows:

| | |
|---|---|
| *Capoeira é uma arte* | Capoeira is an art |
| *Que o Negro inventou* | That the Black Man invented |
| *Foi na briga de duas zebras* | Out of the dance of two zebras |
| *Que N'golo se criou* | N'golo was created |
| *Chegando aqui no Brasil* | Arriving here in Brazil |
| *Capoeira se chamou....* | It was called capoeira ... |

This theory is contradicted by the fact that there isn't any capoeira in Africa. If capoeira as we know it came from Africa, fully developed, one would think that an unbroken lineage of capoeira would be found there, but this isn't the case. Nor is there evidence of capoeira existing in the African Diaspora.

The art that we know as capoeira today developed in Brazil, but the tradition that it was born from is African. Until recently people did not play a form of capoeira in Africa, but there is evidence in various parts of the continent and African Diaspora of dance/fight/games that resemble capoeira. They are performed inside a circle using acrobatics, cunning, kicks, and take-downs, often accompanied by music and singing. One of the most amazing examples of this comes from Martinique. Modern dancer Katherine Dunham documented a martial art/dance called *Ag'ya* which, like capoeira, is done inside a circle combining *ginga*-like dance moves, acrobatic movements, and kicks that resemble the *meia-lua-de-compasso*, *armada*, and *queixada*. A simple Internet search will yield plenty of video evidence of this.

With this being the case, it is obvious that the seed of capoeira is African, and that it reached maturity in Brazil. It was in Brazil that this general ritual shared by African slaves began to develop into what we know as capoeira today. I believe that the political controversy over the African vs. Brazilian issue is a result of different perspectives. Brazilians say capoeira was created there in Brazil, so it's Brazilian—end of story. Those who tend to define things as being African, not based on the borders of countries in which the invention took place but based on who is doing the inventing, define capoeira as African. It is from this fundamental difference in perspective that this debate continues, and I don't see it ever being settled. I once heard a mestre describe the dilemma of defining capoeira as African or Brazilian with this analogy/question: what nationality is a child who is conceived in Africa by his African parents but is born in Brazil? However you answer that question will determine which side you fall on in the capoeira debate.

What is important to remember is that capoeira did not evolve as a part of one homogeneous lineage. It looked different during different eras and in different regions in Brazil. What contemporary capoeiristas will tell you is this: Capoeira Angola is traditional capoeira, or it is capoeira in its original form. But the capoeira that most people refer to as Capoeira Angola today (especially in the United States) is the Capoeira Angola interpreted by the great Mestre Pastinha. In my travels to Brazil I have met mestres of Capoeira Angola who come from other lineages, and they play Capoeira Angola very differently, including the tempo at which the game is played, and the energy level. I have seen mestres of Capoeira Angola who are part of the same school play and teach capoeira totally differently. Capoeira has never been just one way. It did not come from one master and get passed down from generation to generation to present times. As a result, there are general rituals that are present in all of capoeira, but to say that capoeira is just this way, or just that way, would be incorrect.

What we do know for sure is that the African slaves practiced capoeira in secret. One popular belief as to how the art received its name comes from a method the Africans used to conceal their training. It's believed that the Africans would sneak out into the bush, or the *capoeira*, to discreetly hone their skills in the art.

Hiding in the bush was not the only method used by the Africans to conceal capoeira. The *roda* or playing circle of capoeira is controlled by the *berimbau*, which is a one-string bow instrument from Africa. Capoeiristas play capoeira based upon the rhythm played on the *berimbau*. When the overseers or slave masters, and later the police, came around, a look-out would signal the leaders of the *roda*, and the rhythm played on the *berimbau* would change. This advised the capoeiristas to play a game that was less martial, and to play one that looked more like a dance. This would lead the overseers to believe that the slaves were just dancing and having fun, thus there was no cause to be alarmed.

There are records of capoeira in Rio de Janeiro during slavery, but the northeast became known as the home of capoeira, and particularly its main city, Salvador, in the state of Bahia. Capoeira served as a motivating force for the African slaves to continue fighting their oppression. This fight could be physical, mental, spiritual, and any combination thereof. Due to the resilient spirit of the Africans, capoeira survived slavery. After abolition in Brazil, the now African-Brazilians left the plantations and went to live in the cities, where they were on the lowest rung of the socio-economic ladder. Consequently, the cultural practices that they carried with them were looked down upon, but none more than capoeira because it was perceived to be the most dangerous.

Capoeiristas had long been feared for their fighting prowess. There was a marginalized population of skilled fighters with no money, no jobs, and nowhere to go, living off their wits on the streets. It is during this time period that capoeira became associated with *ladrãos*, or criminals. Capoeiristas were regularly imprisoned, and some accounts state that capoeiristas were killed for playing capoeira or simply being known capoeiristas—the most notable of whom was Besouro Preto. It literally was against the law to practice capoeira.[2] Fortunately, when the authorities stamped capoeira out in one place, it popped up again in another. Capoeira endured this existence until the mid 1930s. It was at this time that Manoel dos Reis Machado, the infamous Mestre Bimba, created Capoeira Regional and opened the first capoeira academy of any kind. It was largely the work of Mestre Bimba that brought capoeira from the underground to the forefront of Brazilian society.

Mestre Bimba's objective was to gain respect for the art of capoeira, which by that point had been demonized and outlawed. Mestre Bimba developed a system of teaching capoeira and named it *"Luta Regional Baiana,"* meaning "Bahian Regional Fight." Bimba's approach to capoeira, which became referred to simply as *Regional* (pronounced hay-gee-o-nal), was more

Professor Tartaruga, Mestre João Grande, Rolo

martial arts-oriented because he thought that capoeira had become too folkloric and lost its martial application. Before this, there was one name for capoeira, but once Bimba began teaching his Regional, other capoeiristas began calling capoeira as they knew it Capoeira Angola to differentiate it from Regional and to show respect to the oral tradition that capoeira originated in *N'golo.*

Bimba's approach gained respect quickly because of his reputation as a great fighter. Bimba issued a challenge to all the different martial artists around Bahia to try their skills against his. Some accepted the challenge, but none were victorious. There arose a political push to promote capoeira as the first true Brazilian sport, and consequently Mestre Bimba received official licensing for his academy in 1937 (it had been open since 1932). In effect, capoeira became legal.

A few years later Mestre Pastinha (Vincent Ferreira Pastinha), one of the great masters in the history of capoeira, opened the first Capoeira Angola academy. Capoeira then began to be taught in formal settings, instead of just having a few apprentices. With the advent of the academy, a master could now teach twenty, thirty, or maybe even fifty students at a time by offering several classes a day.

At this point, capoeira spread like wildfire through Brazilian popular culture beyond Salvador, beyond the northeast of Brazil, and did not stop until it had enveloped most of the country. It was not long until the beauty of this great art spread beyond the borders of Brazil and arrived in various other countries. It arrived here in the United States in the 1970s. The first master to come to the U.S. was Mestre Jelon Viera, who began teaching in New York. Capoeira has since spread to countless cities in the United States and all over the world. The great Mestre João Grande, a student of Mestre Pastinha, once told me that capoeira is like the sun and belongs to whoever receives its rays.

## Notes

1. John Lowell Lewis, *Ring of Liberation: Deceptive Discourse in Brazilian Capoeira* (Chicago, IL: University of Chicago Press, 1992), p. 43.

2. Ibid., p. 44.

# 2

# The Roda

The *roda*, which means "the circle," *is* capoeira. A student can learn to throw a kick, to dodge an attack, or to do a cartwheel, but those are just movements until they can be done in the *roda*, in play with another person. A hundred years ago the *roda* was the only place to learn capoeira. When Mestre Bimba, or Pastinha, or Caiçara learned to play capoeira, they had to get in the *roda* to do so. Many students now train several classes a week or even several classes a day. Intense training is beneficial and is encouraged, but anyone who knows anything about capoeira knows that the best capoeiristas are those who play in the *roda* frequently.

Some may think that capoeiristas who frequently play in the *roda* do so because they are already proficient. That is not the case. In my experience, the capoeiristas who develop rapidly are those who have the courage to jump in the *roda*. Training in class supplements the *roda*, but it can never be a substitute for it. Training in class is vital for conditioning your body, building motor coordination, developing reflexes, etc., but it is only 10% of your learning. The other 90% takes place in the *roda*. Nothing can substitute for the energy of the *roda*. So what makes the *roda* so special? Why does it account for such a vast majority of your learning?

Let us first go back to its name: *roda*. As previously stated, the word *roda* means "circle." Throughout history the circle has been considered a special shape, and as a result it holds a special significance in capoeira. A circle is the perfect shape. It has no beginning and no end. It is a symbol of unity and equality. When capoeiristas form a circle, they are creating their own world. The *roda* is closed, and all the energy produced inside it is contained therein, serving to benefit all members of the *roda*. This energy is separate from that outside the *roda*, and consequently it is vital to keep the circle unbroken. I often tell my students that the *roda* is a living and breathing thing. It has a spirit of its own, and those of us who comprise the *roda* are its organs and body parts. The generation of good energy in the *roda* is the responsibility of the mestre or the person leading the *roda* and should be watched over carefully. It's also the responsibility of everyone in the *roda* to contribute to the generation of this energy.

The way the *roda* works is as follows: You have a *bateria*, or set of instruments (a pick-up band), that includes varying combinations of *berimbaus* (the stringed instruments), an *atabaque* (drum), *pandeiros* (tambourines), an *agogô* (cowbell), and a *reco-reco* (a ridged, washboard-like instrument). Of the *berimbaus*, there are three types: the *gunga* (deep-pitched), the *medio* (medium-pitched), and the *viola* (high-pitched). These instruments are aligned in varying formations from group to group but are always considered the head of the *roda*.

All energy in the *roda* comes forth from the *bateria*, and the *bateria* is led by the *gunga berimbau*. The person playing the *gunga* is generally the mestre or the person responsible for the *roda*, and the rhythm that they play on the *berimbau* is followed by the rest of the *bateria*. The *gunga* determines the pace of game, style of game, and when a game begins and ends. The energy produced by the *bateria* is what the *roda* feeds off, and the music of capoeira is what makes it capoeira: without the music, it's just movements.

When the *roda* begins, the first sound heard is that of the *gunga berimbau*, and then the accompanying instruments in the *bateria*. From there a *ladainha* ("litany" or traditional prayer) or other appropriate song is launched to set the energy for the *roda*, to remind the capoeiristas of old mestres, to tell a story, or to convey some other message. One of my favorite *ladainhas* was written by Mestre Pastinha:

| | |
|---|---|
| *Maior é Deus* | God is great |
| *Maior é Deus* | God is great |
| *Pequeno sou eu* | I am small |
| *Tudo que eu tenho* | All that I have |
| *Foi Deus que me deu* | It was God that gave it to me |
| *A roda da capoeira* | The *roda* of Capoeira |
| *Grande, pequeno sou eu* | is big, I am small |
| *Camara ...* | Comrade ... |

After the *ladainha*, songs are recited, and they are absolutely vital to having an animated *roda*. The songs can admonish the capoeiristas in the *roda* for playing too aggressively, they can encourage them to take their game up a notch, or a song can be improvised to give up-to-the-second commentary on what's taking place in the *roda*. If a capoeirista is playing a remarkable game someone might sing:

| | |
|---|---|
| *O menino é bom* | The boy is good |
| *Bate palmas 'pra ele* | Clap your hands for him |
| *O menino é bom* | The boy is good |
| *Bate palmas 'pra ele* | *Clap your hands for him (chorus)* |
| *Sabe jogar* | He knows how to play |
| *Bate palmas 'pra ele* | *Clap your hands for him (chorus)* |
| *A jogar capoeira* | To play capoeira |
| *Bate palmas 'pra ele* | *Clap your hands for him (chorus)* |

As another example, if the tempo in the *roda* has been slow and the mestre is ready to pick it up, then he might sing:

| | |
|---|---|
| *Cuidado menino o som vai subir* | Be careful, boy, the music is going to speed up |
| *Os filhos de Bimba não podem cair* | The sons of Bimba can't fall |
| *Cuidado menino o som vai subir* | *Be careful, boy, the music is going to speed up (chorus)* |
| *Os filhos de Bimba não podem cair* | The sons of Bimba can't fall |

After the *roda* has begun and the energy has been set, the mestre gives permission to the waiting capoeiristas to begin playing. Two capoeiristas enter the *roda* from the *pé do berimbau* ("foot" of the berimbau) and begin their game. Everyone in the *roda* is singing the chorus to whatever song is being led, clapping their hands, and focused on what's taking place in the *roda*. This is very important! If you are not playing an instrument in the *bate-*

Professor Tartaruga and Mestre Ralil

*ria*, or inside the *roda* playing capoeira, you are still a vital part of the *roda*.

I never pass up the opportunity to point out to my students that you can't make a *roda* by yourself. You can get as good as you want at capoeira, but you can't form a circle, play all the instruments in the *bateria*, lead the songs, respond with the chorus, and play a game in the *roda* all by yourself. Everyone has to pitch in and do their part to generate and maintain good energy in the *roda*. I call people who stand in the *roda* but don't sing and clap along with everyone else "leeches." That's exactly what they are. They expect to go in the *roda* and benefit from the energy generated by everyone else, but then aren't willing to help keep that energy going for others. They are the annoying friend who always comes to your house to eat but is never around when it's time to cook or clean up.

The goal of the two capoeiristas in the *roda* is to always play to the music. Their game should be a dialogue or a conversation, but not one spoken with words. Instead, their vocabularies consist solely of the movements of capoeira. The temperament of the conversation should coincide with the rhythm being played by the *berimbau*. There are several rhythms that we use in Raízes do Brasil capoeira (my group), namely: *Angola, Benguela, São Bento Pequeno, São Bento Grande de Angola, São Bento Grande de Bimba* (also called *São Bento Corrido*), *Santa Maria,* and *Iúna*. So, if *Benguela* is being played by the *berimbau,* then the dialogue in the *roda* should be fluid, clean, continuous, and not brutish. If *Iúna* is being played, the dialogue should be graceful and acrobatic, demonstrating superior skill. (Note: *Iúna* is used only for graduated students and above.) But if the rhythm is *São Bento Grande de Bimba,* then the dialogue should be fast-paced, explosive, and objective, i.e., no feigned attacks.

Regardless of the rhythm being played, the game should always be spontaneous, and the two capoeiristas should maintain continuous motion. Capoeira does not have predetermined moves. There is no set response to any given attack. Any technique is appropriate if applied with the proper timing and given the proper circumstances. This is what makes good capoeira so attractive to the spectator. I have frequently been asked by onlookers after street *rodas* or performances if capoeira is rehearsed or choreographed. I smile and humbly tell them no.

Martial arts in general are rhythmic. If you block a punch in karate, there is a rhythm to it. If you block too soon or too late—meaning you are off-beat—you will be punched right in the face. With this in mind, the music of capoeira has an added benefit beyond folklore. Learning to play while listening and conforming to the rhythm of the instruments develops a heightened since of timing, which when used for martial applications can be lethal. There is a defense for any attack, but there is no defense for the proper attack applied with the proper timing.

# 3

# Attitude and Etiquette

Let's return to the importance of actually playing in the *roda*. Training set combinations in class will give you the repetitive work needed to learn the mechanics of a movement, but it will not teach you how to execute that movement. If I know exactly what my training partner is going to do and when he is going to do it (as when training set combinations in class), I can execute almost any movement, but if I have no clue as to what he is going to do next (like when playing inside the *roda*), then my job becomes more challenging.

If I were to stand there waiting for my partner to do something so I could then pounce, it would be considered bad form and ugly— in capoeira you should always be moving and striving for *"o jogo bonito"* or "the beautiful game." The type of game previously mentioned is called *Boca de Espera* or "The Waiting Mouth," meaning you are sitting there waiting with your mouth open for your opportunity to attack. A capoeirista playing *Boca de Espera* deteriorates the quality of game in the *roda*. He doesn't challenge himself to be spontaneous and misses out on opportunities to discover new things. Additionally, he limits the game of his opponent because his opponent can't perform any movement without being taken advantage of. This leads to an annoying exchange of countless fakes and a lot of waiting. The end result of this type of game is always ugly, and unfortunately leads to many fights. Aggression is a natural occurrence because when you play *Boca de Espera* you threaten and put your opponent on guard. The opportunity for graceful spontaneity vanishes and is replaced by force-on-force exchanges.

Remember, capoeira was born in slavery and was an art form of the meek. The inventors of capoeira were overworked and malnourished. So good capoeira, though deadly, isn't based on force. A capoeirista should be able to hide his or her intentions while waiting for an opening to appear, or even manipulate the opponent into a particular situation, thereby creating the opening. Once that opening appears, a capoeirista should be able to instantly recognize it and pounce with the appropriate attack. I always tell my students that as capoeiristas they should move like cats. I say this because all cats are light on their feet, spring into action, and are extremely quick.

When I say that a capoeirista should be able to manipulate opponents into a particular situation, we are talking about a key aspect of capoeira: *mandinga*. The term comes from African spiritual beliefs and signifies magical power. *Mandinga* is related to capoeira because a good capoeirista is able to manipulate their opponents in the *roda*. This manipulation isn't anything magical. It's being adept at anticipating your opponent's next move and taking advantage of it. Capoeira is like chess in that you want to think two, three, and four movements ahead. If you are able to do this, then you have *mandinga*. You will regularly create a situation that places your opponents at your mercy.

Playing with *mandinga* isn't using your muscles, but your brain. Your brain is more important than any muscle used while playing capoeira. I preach to my students to always be thinkers. Always watch while others are in the *roda*. Try to look for openings that the two people in the *roda* are taking advantage of, or openings that they missed. Ask yourself when one player catches another player with a particular movement, how did they accomplish that? Then ask yourself how the other player could have escaped.

With all the exercising that we do, capoeira is still far more of a mental game than a physical game. We condition our bodies to enable them to keep up with our minds. I can't tell you how many times I have seen opportunities but didn't have the explosion, quickness, or flexibility to take advantage of them. I have often come up with new movements while driving down the street, but once I get to the academy, I am unable to execute them due to physical limitations. So capoeiristas must condition their bodies—increase their flexibility, endurance, strength, balance, etc.—but all this is done so that the body is capable of doing what the mind can conceive.

An additional mental concept fundamental to the game of capoeira is *malícia*. This literally translates to "malice" but is perhaps better described in English as "cunning" when one's intention is not premeditated evil. *Malícia*, as it relates to capoeira, has to do with the awareness of potential traps that may be set by your opponent. A capoeirista must have a keen level of alertness. You must sense what your opponent is trying to do and counter his plans effectively.

While learning how to play with *malícia*, you can't forget another fundamental concept that is present in all types of capoeira games: continuity. Capoeira requires a delicate balance of the mind and body. I have just written about how important your mind is in capoeira, but you can't get lost inside your own head. No capoeirista will be instantly adept at playing with *mandinga* and *malícia*. These abilities are acquired through time and experience, for which there is no substitute. You have to pay your dues, so to speak. All too often I have seen capoeiristas who are new to the art and ambitious. They might have read a book or two on capoeira, or maybe heard someone talk about the concepts of *mandinga* and *malícia,* and they try to master these concepts instantly. Trying to be an overnight *mandigueiro* (someone with *mandinga)* is a futile and dangerous endeavor. Students who attempt this become paralyzed by their minds. They start to think too much and are unable to be spontaneous. A capoeirista has to make decisions in a split second and have it be the right decision. What art form, from martial arts to oil painting, do you know of that can be mastered in a month? I have seen students get so frustrated by not being able to perfect something right away. I don't try to squash their ambition to progress, but I try to encourage them to be patient. You have to play your game, make some mistakes, study what went wrong, and learn from it. There is no other process for learning capoeira. There is a song in capoeira that goes:

| | |
|---|---|
| *Na vida se cai,* | In life you will fall |
| *Se leva rasteira* | If you are swept off of your feet |
| *Quem nunca caiu* | He who hasn't fallen |
| *não é capoeira* | is not a capoeirista |

The moral of the story is this: It's inevitable that everyone is going to get caught while playing capoeira. So don't obsess over *mandinga* and *malícia*. If you train hard and play a lot, these things will naturally develop.

A major hindrance to students being able to take their lumps in stride is a lack of humility. A good capoeirista must be humble. An over-inflated ego will make it difficult to receive basic instructions, inhibiting your progress. Simple lessons will go unlearned, and you will keep bumping into the same obstacles until you humble yourself to whatever it is that capoeira is trying to teach you.

I always laugh to myself when I am teaching something new to my students and one of them gets frustrated if they can't do it perfectly right away. Some things can't be learned immediately. Some things you have to be introduced to, train them for a while, then correct a few things, and after an investment of time you will have learned them. Whenever I see a student struggling with this, I always say, "This is why we come to class. If you had already mastered capoeira then you wouldn't need to be here." You must be able to humble yourself and accept that you aren't going to learn everything immediately.

Now, I am not talking about being lazy and not working hard to execute particular techniques. That is something altogether different. I am talking about not worrying about who is watching, or how you might look to your fellow classmates, and being fully engaged in the learning process. Try, fail, try again, fail again, improve, try some more, make a couple more mistakes, learn some more, then accomplish your goal. Students frequently ask me what exactly they should be working on to improve their game. For my more advanced students I generally will explain what deficiencies I have noticed in their games, but to my newer students my response is simple, "Keep coming to class."

When I first began to teach, I had a student come through my class who was interesting, to say the least. He was a break dancer, had trained martial arts when he was a kid, and he had amazing athletic talent. I instantly recognized that this guy had the physical potential to be an amazing capoeirista.

He approached me after one class to ask me for some pointers. I was happy to help. I love it when my students ask questions. Nothing makes me happier because it means that they are actually thinking about capoeira. It shows me that they are processing information and trying to understand what it is they are doing. It irks me to no end when I know that people did not fully grasp the training, yet they have no questions when I inquire if anything is unclear. So when this young man asked me to give him some pointers I was eager to comply. I asked, "What do you need help with?"

I will never forget his response. He told me, "I already know capoeira. I mean, I've been break dancing since I was a kid so I already know all the movements, I just need you to show me how to do them inside the roda."

If this were to happen today I would walk away immediately, but I was new to teaching, so I actually tried to explain to him how the two are different. He cut me off, insisting, "Capoeira and break dancing are the same. Just show me how to mix the moves in with my ginga." At this point, I took my cue to end the conversation.

This young man was lacking humility. He couldn't humble himself to receive basic instructions. Break dancing was inspired by capoeira but is a totally different art form. The similarities between the two arts are found primarily in their acrobatic movements. When this guy couldn't hear that simple fact, I knew he wasn't ready to be a student—or, shall I say, he wasn't ready to be my student. He kept coming to class and he struggled due to his misconception. After a while he became frustrated watching students with far less talent begin to progress in ways that he wasn't. I hoped the lesson that kept smacking him in the face would sink in. Unfortunately it didn't, and he soon quit. The fundamental problem was that the guy simply was not humble. A lack of humility leads to a wealth of problems in the capoeira world in general, and in the *roda* in particular.

One of the major problems that a lack of humility spawns is overly violent capoeira games. These altercations aren't even games. They go beyond capoeira and degenerate to flat-out fights. You don't know how many times I have seen two capoeiristas playing in the *roda*, when one person executes a beautiful *rasteira* (a sweep), and the game immediately intensifies. Both players begin playing at a tempo far faster than the rhythm. They wear their intentions on their sleeves. Nothing is disguised, fluidity vanishes, and what was once a game becomes pure aggression. This was all set in motion by a simple *rasteira*. Aren't *rasteiras* a part of the game?

The problem is that a lot of capoeiristas can't control their ego. Few things are more beautiful than when one capoeirista gets caught with a *rasteira*, and without losing his cool he returns to the game; then at the right time later in the game he returns the favor by executing a *rasteira* on his opponent. I have seen the participants of *rodas* nearly tear the roof off a building with excitement, appreciative spectators cheering and yelling when two players challenge each other while staying within the game of capoeira and trading clean, cleverly disguised attacks.

One of my mestre's more famous quotes is, "Capoeira is the only game that can have two winners." He says this because if you receive a *cabeçada* (head butt), the game isn't over. You have not lost. The game goes on, and you and your opponent should continue to build a beautiful dialogue. If before the game ends you are able to execute a *tesoura* (scissors take-down) on your opponent, who won the game? The answer is both of you.

One of the best games that I ever played was with a good friend of mine, Professor Tereu (Teles Renato). People were in Oakland from all over the country for a *batizado* I was hosting, plus Mestre Ralil, Mestre Pablo, and Contramestre Foca from Brazil. We were playing *São Bento Grande de Bimba* (which means we were playing at a fast pace), and in the middle of the game Tereu caught me with a *rasteira* that almost made me fall. I was barely able to spin out without falling, and as I spun I countered with a *meia-lua-de-compasso*. He barely dodged the kick, and our exchange continued with attacks and counter-attacks. The people in the *roda* were yelling and cheering. Both of our mestres were in the *roda* watching (Tereu is a student of Mestre Pablo), and nothing motivates a capoeirista to demonstrate dominance more than the watchful eyes of his mestre. Tereu and I both put our respective egos to the side and just enjoyed the game. Both of us were smiling from ear to ear during the entire game. Finally, after Tereu almost kicked me with a *gancho*, he and I did a *volta ao mundo*. People were hopping around the *roda*, the *bateria* was playing beautifully, Mestre Ralil was singing a song that had everyone animated, and every single person was clapping to the beat.

Tereu and I returned to the *pé do berimbau* and were prepared to keep playing. At this point I am sure that 95% of the people in the *roda* expected us to come out again and try to tear each other's head off. Dripping in sweat and still smiling, we both entered the *roda:* he with his trademark back flip that looks like he is in the movie *The Matrix,* and I with an *armada dupla.* From there we played a game that was equally exciting and engaged, but it was mainly filled with hand spins, head spins, flips, and other acrobatic movements, all the while looking for an opening to attack.

Tereu and I both sensed what was happening. The intensity of the game had gone up and up, but when we did a *volta ao mundo* the game was still a game. It hadn't become overly aggressive; it had remained fluid and spontaneous and still had a hint of playfulness. Without saying a word to each other, we had decided at the *berimbau* that we were going to change things up a little. So when we returned to the *roda*, we took our games up to another level, and not down to punches and kicks to the knees.

All too often games like this take a turn for the worse. I almost fell from that first *rasteira;* too many capoeiristas in a similar situation would begin to play *Boca de Espera* and devolve the game. I myself have been guilty of this in the past, at times when I wasn't able to let the *rasteira* go. Sometimes you just get caught. Sometimes you won't be able to counter and catch your opponent, and that's okay. I look at it like this: when I simply sweep someone I am not challenging them to a fight. I'm not talking about kicking their leg out from underneath them with brute force, leaving a bruise. I am talking about executing a *rasteira* with proper timing and minimal force. If this is the case, then when someone sweeps me, they are not challenging me to a fight either.

Being overly competitive can only inhibit you in capoeira.

Admittedly, there are non-humble capoeiristas who can play capoeira very well. They are overly violent and sometimes downright mean. I think these capoeiristas are both dangerous and bad for capoeira. Their mentality results in a lot people getting hurt and countless others having a bad impression of capoeira.

Once when I was in Brazil training, we had a *roda* at my mestre's academy. The games had gotten pretty tough, with one capoeirista in particular trying to challenge everyone he played in an overly aggressive manner. That night at dinner Mestre Ralil and I discussed the *roda*. Inevitably the conversation arrived at the topic of this particular capoeirista. I said something to the effect that the guy was tough, but Mestre Ralil responded, "It's not toughness, it is insecurity." His words were simple but profound. Insecurities ranging from manhood issues, past abuse and/or class consciousness to concerns over which group is the "best" cause many capoeiristas to be unnecessarily violent.

My students know that fistfights are not allowed in my *roda*, but nonetheless their tempers flare every now and again. To expect otherwise would be unrealistic on my part. Watching different students battle with this over the years, I have come to learn that the more humble you are, the easier it is to learn capoeira. I was watching a movie recently with a line that roughly went, "Vanity and happiness are in direct contradiction." I laughed to myself because I have seen this so many times in capoeira. I have seen students with the whole world available to them, if they could only humble themselves.

One particular student comes to mind. He is talented, sharp mentally, coordinated, and strong. But he is overly concerned with his image. I have watched in pure frustration over the years as this same issue continues to limit his growth. I have known other individuals who are exceptional capoeiristas and could be truly great, but they are insecure and lack humility. As a consequence they are overly violent. One thing I learned at a young age: no matter how bad you might be, there is always someone out there badder than you. I have seen capoeiristas barred from participating in events because of their reputations, and even worse, I have seen capoeiristas ambushed for the same reason. People like this cultivate a gang mentality in capoeira. Personally, I am trying to use capoeira to take kids away from gangs, not to turn them into thugs.

I am fully aware that capoeira is also a martial art. I am not trying to turn capoeira into patty-cake. People who try to do this probably should study another art form. I just happen to believe that there is a limit to what should be done in the *roda*.

Certain aspects of capoeira are meant for your self-defense on the streets, and not to seriously injure others inside the *roda*. In a conversation with Mestre Nenel, the son of Mestre Bimba, in which we talked about violence in capoeira, his take on it was that capoeira is not war. If it is, then why do we have instruments and why are we singing? He said war has no rules and uses weapons; capoeira is something else.

So if we go back to our original question of why does 90% of a capoeirista's learning take place in the *roda*, the answer should now be clear: Situations arise that can't be simulated in training. Eventually all capoeiristas have to get off the bench and on the playing field. It is often said that the *roda* is like life: watching others live their lives isn't living yours.

# 4

# Philosophies of Capoeira

*A volta que o mundo deu, a volta que mundo da:* Roughly translated, this saying means "What I give the world, the world gives back to me." It's a little bit like "what goes around comes around." This is one of the oldest principles in any society. Most people nowadays call it karma. The message is that we should be mindful of what we do.

If you are playing in the *roda* and you recognize an opportunity to strike someone, you should be mindful of this principle. Why are you going to strike your opponent? Is this a situation when you should just mark your attack? If you do strike your opponent, are you striking them with excessive force or bad intentions? I ask these questions because once you set something in motion, you can't take it back.

For example: Let's say that two capoeiristas are playing in the *roda,* and maybe there are a lot of people watching. One player *rasteiras* (sweeps) the other. The capoeirista who received the *rasteira* could become embarrassed. The game continues and the capoeirista who received the *rasteira* gets an opening to deliver a *martelo* to his opponent's face. Remember, his ego was bruised by getting dropped on his butt with a *rasteira.* Everyone in the *roda* laughed and cheered when it happened. If you are this capoeirista, what do you do at this moment? Whatever decision you make, you are going to be accountable for the consequences.

This principle of *a volta que o mundo deu* is tied into one of my favorite lyrics in capoeira: " *Quem não pode com mandinga, não carrega patuá.*" Translated, the lyric says, "If you can't handle the magic, then don't wear the amulet." Stated another way, if you can't handle the consequences, then don't commit the action.

Going back to the previous example, let's say the capoeirista takes his opportunity to deliver a *martelo* to his opponent's face with full force, and he knocks his opponent flat out. What are the consequences of his action? Some folks in the *roda* may admire him for being tough. Some may think he is a jerk and want to teach him a lesson when they get the chance to play with him. The beginning students in the *roda* might become intimidated, and as a result not want to play with him or develop a relationship with him. And we still have to contend with the guy who took the *martelo* to the face. What is he going to do—after he wakes up?

In the beginning of the game he gave you a *rasteira*, which is a fundamental goal in capoeira. Giving a *rasteira* is like shooting a jump shot in basketball or hitting a home run in baseball. It is not cause to start a fight. But since you kicked your opponent in the face, I guarantee you that he now has a score to settle with you. Be prepared! The conflict that now exists wasn't necessary. Nonetheless, it is now very real and it's a result of what you set in motion. The world will give back to you what you gave it.

Two students who train with me have an interesting history together. One is more graduated than the other, and he would unnecessarily provoke the less graduated student. In basic terms, he would bully him. The more graduated student had given something to the world. The less graduated student trained diligently and continued to improve. The games that the two of them played went from being ones in which the more graduated student was bullying the less graduated student, to something resembling a dispute between equal capoeiristas. With time, the less graduated student became a superior capoeirista. As you might expect, he hadn't forgotten any of the past incidents in which the more graduated student bullied him. Fortunately for the more graduated student, I didn't allow my *rodas* to be excessively violent. I say this because the (formerly) less graduated student challenged him at every turn, and if I allowed it, he would have hurt him.

So what do you take from this into your everyday life? Be conscious of how you treat people. Don't take what doesn't belong to you. When you are in a position of power, be fair in your dealings. What you send into the world will come back to you. Some call it karma, chickens coming home to roost, or justice. It goes by many names, but the idea is the same: treat people how you would like to be treated.

*Cair no rolê:* Roughly translated as "fall into a roll," this means that when you get knocked off your feet, don't fall flat on your back. Capoeiristas are supposed to be adept at this. In the game of capoeira only five parts of the body should touch the ground:

your two hands, your two feet, and your head. If while playing a game of capoeira you lose your balance, or someone helps you to lose your balance, you are not to fall flat. With still only your hands, feet, or head being allowed to touch the ground, you are supposed to improvise, adapt, and roll smoothly out of the fall and return to the game. This is one of the mini games within a game.

This principle teaches you how to handle adversity. Times are not always going to be nice. Times are not always going to be easy. Who would want that anyway? Anyone who has ever experienced adversity of any kind knows the tough times make the good times that much more enjoyable. With adversity being a given in life, we need to be capable of dealing with it. Some people simply give up and fall flat when they are knocked off balance, while others try to fight the fact that they are even off balance. Neither response is good. Ideally, you would like to perceive the threat and avoid it, but some things catch you off guard. When this happens you must be able to react quickly and continue moving forward.

*Malícia:* This is probably the most important attribute of an adept capoeirista. To have *malícia* is to have a high level of alertness and keen perception. As a philosophy, capoeiristas should walk through their lives constantly utilizing this principle.

I once heard a notable capoeira mestre describe *malícia* through the metaphor of a suspicious cat. If anyone has ever seen a cat approach a situation it isn't sure of, that is *malícia* personified. Cats don't rush into situations that they aren't familiar with. They slowly approach the object of their curiosity, extremely cautious, and they try to detect all potential dangers.

Playing capoeira without *malícia* isn't playing capoeira. With capoeira being a game of constant improvisation and creativity, you must be ready to detect and react to all traps that your opponent may try to lure you into. As previously stated, the trick is to do this without breaking your flow. Capoeiristas should be in constant motion while playing, so it's not acceptable for a capoeirista to become paralyzed by fear or paranoia. Consequently, in order to truly be adept, a capoeirista must have a heightened level of *malícia*.

The benefit of *malícia* in your life outside the *roda* is directly related to your well-being. In life danger can come from many directions and in many forms. A frightening and (now) hilarious story from my own life that parallels this—it occurred when I first traveled to Brazil. I had flown down with a crew of my fellow capoeiristas, and the first city we visited was Rio de Janeiro. Here in the United States pedestrians have the right of way. Now I don't pretend to know the penal code in Rio de Janeiro, but I do know that functionally there is no such thing as pedestrian rights. The streets belong to the cars, and if a pedestrian wants to step off the sidewalk and onto the street, he must do so at his own risk.

So there I was: It was my first day in a distant land, with different customs, and I was coming from the Bay Area in California where everyone jay-walks. We weren't off the plane two hours before we were walking down Rua Voluntarios da Pátria, which is a major street in the neighborhood of Botafogo. We came to an intersection with a small residential street. Me being the *gringo* (non-Brazilian) that I am, I just stepped off the curb. At the same time a car came zipping down the street, turning onto Rua Voluntarios da Pátria, and it almost took half of me with it.

That car came so close to hitting me that I still can't believe it didn't. If I had been using *malícia*, I would have never come so close to being hit. I would have noticed the car zipping down the street and would have perceived the behavior of the local pedestrians; consequently I would have known to keep my butt on the curb where it was safe until the light was green.

Like I said before, there are countless forms of danger out there in the world. They can come from anywhere at any time. Capoeira teaches you to perceive these dangers and, without becoming paralyzed by fear or paranoia, to keep yourself safe.

*Esquiva:* The literal translation of *esquiva*, pronounced es-kee-va, is "to evade." *Esquiva* is the basic defense to any attack in capoeira, and the basic concept is to evade the attack by accompanying it or "going with it" not against it. Put another way, don't fight force with force. In capoeira we don't block attacks. The goal is to evade the force of your opponent and to counter-attack using your opponent's force against him. This concept is fundamental to capoeira. Today capoeiristas are well nourished; they lift weights, take vitamins and supplements, and are generally stronger than capoeiristas were three hundred years ago. But capoeira was not, and still is not, an art form based upon strength. Remember, capoeira was developed by the meek—individuals who were malnourished and overworked. Consequently, the

Pente

strategies of capoeira are based on using your attacker's force against him instead of meeting that force head on.

One of the most beautiful illustrations of this is when a petite woman executes a *rasteira* on a large man delivering a powerful attack. I have seen countless women, undersized and outmatched physically, put larger brutish men flat on their backs. The basic concept is that your force increases exponentially when you use your opponent's force against him. This concept can be applied in any situation when you are being attacked, whether it is an argument, chess, or basketball. You might even encourage your opponent's aggressiveness in order to lure them into a well-conceived trap.

*Dois Vencedores (Two Winners):* The game of capoeira is probably the most difficult martial art to judge because so many elements are mixed into one big pot of *feijoada* (traditional bean stew). Consequently, capoeira is the only game in which you can have two winners.

One of the most memorable games I have ever seen take place happened right in my academy. Two of my students, "Pente" and "Mel," were playing a great game. Out of nowhere it seemed, Pente executed a perfect *tesoura* (scissors take-down) on Mel. Mel was caught completely off guard, but as a great capoeirista should, she regained her bearings quickly. Pente tried to exit the *tesoura* with an *aú* (cartwheel), but Mel caught him in the middle of his *aú* with a *cabeçada* that toppled him over onto his back. So who won this game? You can't definitively say that Pente or Mel won; they both were winners.

The subtle message in this aspect of capoeira can't be stressed enough. All too often in life we approach each other as adversaries. It shouldn't be that way. Use your life experiences to learn and improve yourself. I don't know exactly which old philosopher is credited with the saying, but it's often repeated that sometimes when you win you actually lose. Your biggest adversary is within. If you spend all your time combating others, you won't ever face your biggest opponent: yourself! Additionally, when you are always competing with the outside world you can end up comparing yourself to the lowest common denominator. Put another way, a priest shouldn't compare himself to the behavior of criminals. He should hold himself to a higher standard (the Bible), but if he's looking for validation by comparing himself to his environment, he can have a false sense of accomplishment.

*Harmonia:* The concept of harmony is prevalent in capoeira, but it is often overlooked. How can this be? One of the most fundamental aspects of capoeira has passed this principle on from generation to generation: music. The *bateria* of the roda sets everything in motion harmoniously. The *gunga, medio, viola, atabaque, pandeiro, agogô, reco-reco,* the hand claps, and the songs must fluidly come together in unison. No aspect can go off on its own tangential path on a whim. Instead, all parts must work together to accomplish one end: good energy in the *roda*. From time to time we all feel out of whack, off balance, or frustrated. In life, as in the *roda*, we must have attuned senses to recognize when something is out of order or is in conflict with our goal(s), and then be able to set it right.

As a "raw cord" (a term for a novice player who hasn't yet graduated to a higher level indicated by a system of colored cords/belts), I couldn't truly appreciate how powerful the harmony of the *bateria* is. Later as an instructor I remember handing the *berimbau* off to one of my students so that I could play in the *roda*. Halfway through my game, my student lost the rhythm and the *bateria* descended into chaos. I immediately *felt* the disharmony and had to do a *volta ao mundo* in order to give the *bateria* time to get itself together.

Through diligent study I became aware of how all the components of the *bateria* are supposed to relate to one another. In parallel, I believe that one of the most worthwhile pursuits in life is to come to understand your thoughts, ambitions, and impulses as they relate to the man or woman you want to be, and to always keep them in harmony with each other as you work towards becoming your ideal self. When an impulse arises, be sure that it adds to the positive energy you are trying to cultivate in your life, as opposed to throwing everything off.

# 5

# Techniques and Strategies

As previously stated, capoeira is more of a mental game than a physical game. The intense physical conditioning that good capoeira requires is only necessary so that the body can keep up with the mind. The essence of capoeira is the matching of wits of the two players in the *roda*. This being the case, a capoeirista's thought process must be developed so that he can create opportunities, recognize them when they appear, and exploit them once they are recognized. I teach three main concepts in order to build a strategic mind: yielding to force, stealing time, and counter-attacking.

The first and most basic concept is yielding to force. This is a relatively natural reflex. If a boulder came rolling down the hill in your direction, you would instinctively step out of its path. Likewise in martial arts, if a strike is launched in your direction, you would evade this attack. Sounds simple enough, so why are we even talking about it? The answer is because what the average person would do instinctively isn't always the most efficient strategically. For example, if your opponent throws a *martelo*, your natural untrained reflex would be to step back out of range of the attack.

If you were to do this, you would be safe. You would have evaded an attack by yielding to your opponent's force. But would you have been efficient in your use of motion? If you notice in the photo, when you step back out of range of your opponent's attack, you are safe from being struck. On the other hand, you weren't able to strike your opponent, either.

There are more efficient ways of yielding to your opponent's force. The most basic is *esquiva*—parallel, front, diagonal, or lateral. Let's revisit the above scenario, but this time we will yield to the opponent's attack with a front *esquiva*.

As you can see, we yield to the attack, letting it harmlessly pass by, but notice how we maintain proximity to our opponent. In the first response to the attack, the defender left the game by retreating to a safe distance where no interaction was possible, but in the second response we see the defender maintaining a safe proximity that allows for continuous interaction.

This is taught to all capoeiristas in their first few classes, but it is frequently abandoned. I even see graduated students revert back to their natural instinct of retreating from an attack when they feel intimidated. I concede that there are instances when you do need to escape out of range, but to become a more adept capoeirista you should cultivate the skill of yielding without retreating. One of the many games within the game of capoeira is the quest for dominance of the center of the circle. If you retreat when attacked, your opponent will establish dominance over the center of the circle while you play on the edges. Being forced to the outer limits of the *roda* is not where you want to be. It is said that a mestre can make the *roda* seem like a square

Melissa and Kevin begin in ginga position

Melissa delivers a martelo and Kevin escapes out of range

Kevin evades Melissa's martelo with front esquiva remaining
in striking distance.

and trap you in one of the corners. This is done because they
are adept at dominating the center of the circle while forcing
you to the edge. Once you're forced back to the edges, you can
only go left or right, but mestres being the savvy cobras that
they are will cut off one of your options, leaving you with only
right, or only left. Once this is done, you are done.

Once you have a solid understanding of yielding to attacks,
you have to learn how to "steal time." This concept is crucial
to boxing, karate, kung fu, fencing, or any other martial art. If
you can steal time, your timing will be impeccable. What do I
mean by *stealing time*? If I am attacked and I take one count to
defend, and another count to counter-attack, then it has taken

Melissa executes rasteira on "Rabo" with perfect timing.

me two total counts. But if I defend and attack at the same time, then it has only taken me one count, so in effect I have stolen one count of time. Consequently, my opponent has one less count of time to defend.

A *rasteira* is a perfect illustration of stealing time. When I first teach students to do *rasteira*, they always want to *esquiva* first and let the kick pass. Then once the opponent has finished his kick, they try to execute their *rasteira*. This doesn't work because it takes two counts. Their opponent's foot that they sought to sweep will no longer be there. Since the opponent's kick takes one count, your *rasteira* at most can take only one count. In the photo you can see the proper timing for executing a *rasteira*.

While the opponent is halfway through his attack, the defender is halfway through his *rasteira*. Instead of waiting in *esquiva* for the kick to pass, you steal that time and use it to your advantage by putting your opponent on his back. Being able to steal time in a game of capoeira is vital, especially when trying to neutralize the speed of your opponent if he is faster than you are. Being able to steal time decreases the interval it takes for you to counter-attack, and if enough time is stolen, you can in effect become faster than your opponent.

This brings us to the third concept, which is counter-attacking. Counter-attacking is not simply throwing an attack after your opponent throws one. To do this would be to simply serve yourself up as prey. Counter-attacking instead is a science that combines the two concepts above and adds unleashing your attack at the optimal time, from the optimal position, to receive the optimal result. Every attack has a defense or counter, but the perfect counter-attack has no defense because there isn't any time to defend.

To illustrate my point, let's say your opponent throws a *martelo* with his left foot; you're in *ginga* position with your left foot back, and you want to counter-attack with a *martelo*. A lateral or parallel *esquiva* would suffice to simply evade the attack, but to effectively counter-attack you should use a diagonal *esquiva*.

By doing this you evade your opponent's *martelo*, you steal time by already moving into your counter-attack, and the angle from which you will be counter-attacking is optimal for delivering a timely and powerful counter-*martelo*.

Melissa and Kevin begin in ginga position

Kevin evades Melissa's martelo with diagonal esquiva

An understanding of these three concepts is crucial to strategically thinking your way through a game. They are like the ABCs of learning to play with *malícia* and *mandinga*, which are the hallmarks of a capoeirista. Cultivating these skills through diligence and patience will open up an infinite world of creativity within capoeira that is bound only by your imagination. When I see a student of mine get it, when I can see the light come on, then I know they have begun their journey to develop wisdom in capoeira. I can only pass on knowledge; wisdom has to be acquired by each individual.

# 6

# Capoeira and Commercialism

There are many capoeiristas who have dedicated their lives to being just that. Like a dancer dances or a musician plays music for a living, capoeiristas make capoeira their profession. I understand their passion for capoeira and their wanting to dedicate their time to refinement within the art form. It only makes sense. I dropped out of college to become a full-time capoeirista myself. It's a labor of love no different than that of a painter or a saxophonist.

Achieving greatness in capoeira is an endless endeavor that is truly worthwhile. There is always more to learn. There is always something to improve upon. There is always something that you once did well but have become a little rusty on. This is the nature of practicing an art form that includes martial arts, dance, acrobatics, singing, music, and history all swirled into one. This being the case, capoeiristas are often inspired to dedicate their lives to their beloved capoeira. This presents an interesting problem: capoeira, by its nature and history, is not a tool of capital gain.

Capoeira is an art form of the oppressed, the marginalized, the have-nots, but in order for a teacher of capoeira to earn a livelihood from the art, he or she is going to have to cater to the haves in society. If I am trying to make a living off capoeira, I am not going to work in the inner city. I am not going to work with youth who are living a life of hopelessness. I am not going to work with the young adult who is surrounded by negativity and destruction. I am not going to work in the neighborhood that is fragmented and in need of a unifying and uplifting art, culture, and way of life. There isn't any money in it. Providing an education about life that shows a twelve-year-old how to think their way out of poverty, or providing a pastime that uplifts the spirit of a twenty-one-year-old frustrated by societal barriers, or uniting individuals who live in the same neighborhood isn't profitable.

If capoeira is your livelihood, then it is your business. Now, from a business standpoint, it only makes sense to offer your services to those with money. If you don't, your business will soon close. In fact, if I have a business, I am not only going to offer its services where I can make money, I am going to offer them where I can make the most money. This is the nature of business. But how do we reconcile this with capoeira and its history?

As it stands, the people who are capable of paying for dance and martial art classes of any type are those well above the poverty line. The high price of many capoeira classes locks poor people out of capoeira. As a businessman my response would be, "So what?" But as a capoeirista my response is, "No way."

Let me clarify that capoeira is for everyone—the poorest of the poor all the way to the wealthiest of the wealthy. I don't believe that anyone should be excluded from participating in capoeira. It is an amazing, unifying tool for folks of all types and backgrounds, but capoeira must always remain capoeira. Its heritage must always be kept alive. Its philosophies must always be passed on without being redefined, their historical context disregarded. Capoeira is free to grow and continue to write its ongoing history to include current events, but we can't allow the history of capoeira to be rewritten. Nor can we allow it to be truncated to begin in the early twentieth century. Capoeira, in its essence, is the *ladainha* of the African slave; the struggle for freedom of a shackled man; a tool to uplift the downtrodden.

How do we reconcile this with having capoeira being exclusively offered to those with money?

In my travels to Brazil I met many capoeiristas who make their living from teaching capoeira. Because of numerous factors including cost of living, family structure, and cost of classes, this is possible to do without abandoning capoeira's roots. Simply put, capoeira teachers don't have to charge as much to earn a living in Brazil, so poor kids can still train capoeira.

The United States represents a totally different situation. I have both charged students tuition for lessons, and provided free classes. I believe that payment of some type is not only appropriate but necessary, whether it be monetary or barter. Something that is offered freely is rarely appreciated or given its due respect. Teachers of capoeira deserve to be compensated for their commitment of time, energy, and expertise. The responsibility of being a teacher is serious and extremely demanding.

There are more examples than I care to remember of students I have taught who, because they didn't have to pay in any form for their capoeira lessons, consequently didn't appreciate what they were receiving; such students would attend classes according to their whims. These students had little to no commitment in their capoeira development nor much respect for their teacher, their group, or the art form.

It is common for folks to not appreciate something given to them freely. I remember how much I didn't fully appreciate things as a child that were given me by my mother, but how I cherished those things that I sacrificed and saved my own money to buy. I remember how much food I used to eat when I lived with my mother. I also remember how I learned to conserve food once I went off to college and had to pay for all that I ate.

So, capoeira teachers should get paid for their time, knowledge, and skill. But, and this is a big *but*, if capoeira becomes your profession—especially here in the United States—then the primary emphasis becomes monetary gain and not the integrity of the art. Less energy is given to conveying the messages and stories of Zumbi, of Besouro Manganga, of Lampião; and more energy is given to packaging and presenting capoeira in a form fit for mass consumption. The unpleasant stories of the slave plantations are replaced with stories of sun-filled days spent on the sands of Copacabana Beach.

I will not belabor this point. I will simply conclude with this: it has become customary for capoeiristas in the United States to have to pay $10 to $20 simply to play capoeira while visiting an open *roda* at another capoeira school. I am not talking about taking a class or charging folks to attend a *batizado*. That makes sense. I am talking about paying to play capoeira at a regular open *roda*. One of the fundamentals of capoeira is that capoeiristas from different schools play together. It once was an honor to have capoeiristas visit your school. It is a great opportunity for everyone involved to learn and grow. If a capoeirista plays with the same people day in and day out, their capoeira growth will be stunted. Unfortunately, folks are now charged for this. Under these circumstances, capoeira loses.

# 7

# Capoeira as a Tool of Oppression

How is it that an art form born in oppression, as a means to combat oppression, later becomes used as a tool of would-be oppressors? I don't know if there is anything more ironic. This injustice has affected so many capoeiristas but is hardly ever addressed.

When I first experienced someone trying to use capoeira to oppress others, I thought it was a rare occurrence. But as time passed it became clear to me that many capoeiristas, independent of school and style, were enduring the same fate.

One time while I was attending a capoeira conference, a student posed the question to a visiting mestre: "How do you feel about so many capoeira mestres using capoeira to control their students' personal lives?" The mestre's response was inadequate, but I was happy that someone brought this topic to the forefront. As I looked around at the faces of the capoeiristas in the room, I saw that the question had resonated with them.

What a teacher is, and what a teacher should be, is all too often distinctly different. Teachers should serve as examples of what you aspire to be—in the way they carry themselves and their choice of actions and words. Instead, many teachers serve as examples of what you don't want to become. Their actions should be observed only to learn what not to do. This of course assumes that you are aspiring to be a decent person. I have witnessed a student's love for capoeira, coupled with the esteem they hold their teacher in, used to oppress that very student.

It is my opinion that it is a privilege and honor to be some-one's teacher. It's an authoritative position that comes with a lot of responsibility. When each of my students chose me as their teacher, they bestowed a gift upon me. They placed me in a position to develop a part of who they are. And if they counted themselves as capoeiristas in every aspect of their life, they allowed me to play a major role in shaping their very identity.

I view this as an honor because as a student myself, I refused to train with just anyone. There are many great mestres in the world, but not every mestre is worthy to be my teacher.

When selecting a mestre, and on the other side when accept-ing a student, the decision should be thought out carefully. When I became a student of Mestre Ralil, I had gotten to know him and what he stood for inside and outside capoeira. He played capoeira with the skill and precision of a true mestre, and he produced students who are now on par with the best capoeiris-tas in the world. But beyond the technical game, beyond the flash and glamour, Mestre Ralil is a humble and caring man. I was able to witness his sincere consideration for his students and how they reciprocated, and this spoke much louder about his credentials as a mestre than his game inside the *roda* ever could.

I recall having a discussion with Mestre Edinho regarding Mestre Ralil. I commented on Mestre Ralil's amazing vision

Professor Tartaruga and Mestre Ralil

inside the *roda*, but more impressively how he could apply that vision to the world outside. Situations of group management that appear to be complicated are handled by Mestre Ralil with relative ease. In response, Mestre Edinho agreed, adding that what makes it more profound is Ralil's ability to do it with honesty and justice.

As a student, these are the types of qualities that I hold in high esteem in a teacher, and as a result I chose the mestre that I did. Students should put some thought into this decision. It's not something that should be entered into haphazardly. More times than I would have liked to, I saw students choose a particular teacher, and the teacher prove to be not qualified or of sufficient character, and the end result is a jaded and scarred capoeirista.

I knew a great capoeirista who loved the art. Her game was truly inspiring, and if she had remained in the art form, she would have been a tremendous role model for women. Unfortunately, after having had one too many bad experiences with her mestre, she quit capoeira one day and never returned. She was so turned off by what she experienced that she wanted nothing to do with capoeira on any level.

This is one of countless situations I've heard about or witnessed firsthand in the capoeira world. This troubles me because capoeira, as any martial art should, is meant to give its practitioners the requisite skills to become the person they want to be. In my own life I've experienced the effects of having a great teacher. The tutelage I've received since a teenager when I first began my journey as a martial artist has helped me grow from an angry adolescent who was constantly fighting into a secure man equipped to handle adversity. Of the many stories I know, let's take a quick look at two of them to explore some of the manners in which capoeira is used to oppress its practitioners.

The first story is truly ironic. There was a group of graduated capoeira students who had dedicated themselves to being great capoeiristas. They trained religiously. They were the kind of students any mestre would want to have. Beyond dedication to their training, they supported the group in any way they could. And as they developed as capoeiristas, they wanted more and more to travel to Brazil so they could train and play with their Brazilian counterparts. They wanted to visit the homeland of their beloved capoeira. They had met several visiting mestres through the years and always imagined what it would be like to visit them in Rio de Janeiro, Brasília, Salvador, or elsewhere in Brazil.

After reaching a certain level of proficiency the students felt they were ready. It was at this time that they started talking with their mestre about actually traveling to Brazil. In the beginning he seemed supportive, saying he would take them himself, but he never did. After waiting patiently, the students asked him one day about traveling to Brazil and the mestre flat-out forbade them to go. No explanation was given. The injustice of the mestre's stance was compounded by the fact that he had sent one of their classmates to train in Brazil for three months less than a year before.

The students were upset and confused. They were all adults, blue cords or above, and they were going to spend their own money to go. Beyond that, they couldn't understand why any mestre of capoeira wouldn't want his students to go to Brazil. After deliberating for a while, the students decided that they had every right to come and go as they pleased, so they bought their tickets to Brazil and informed the mestre that they were going.

This incensed him, and he told the students that he counted their actions as a declaration of war. The mestre began talking to the students one on one, trying to intimidate them into backing out of the trip. He even talked with members of their families in an effort to stop them. Nonetheless the students maintained their resolve and traveled to Brazil.

The mestre felt that because he was their mestre, anything that they wanted to do in relation to capoeira had to be approved by him first. And if they didn't submit themselves to his judgment, they weren't fit to be his students. In the end, all nine of the students who went on the trip were expelled from the school. After a while the mestre felt the effect of losing nine graduated students at once and offered them the opportunity to come back. Only three of the nine students returned, two more continued to train capoeira with a different school, and four quit capoeira altogether.

The second story involves one of the most talented female capoeiristas I have ever known. To watch her play was to watch supreme fluidity and grace in motion. Additionally, she was as strong and explosive as many of her male counterparts, giving her an added dimension that a lot of female capoeiristas may lack. In fact, pound for pound, she is one of the strongest people I have ever known. Unfortunately, she had two characteristics that all too often prove to be a problem in capoeira when they should be non-factors: she was a woman, and she had a boyfriend.

I say that her being a woman was an "unfortunate" characteristic in sarcasm, but her being a woman was a problem nonetheless. Women are not taken as seriously in capoeira by some people for many reasons, the biggest of which is they are seen as sexual objects. The culture of capoeira is still overwhelmingly masculine, and oftentimes women practitioners are focused on as potential mates. Regardless of skill, too many male capoeiristas are unable to see female capoeiristas in a platonic light. The situation is compounded when it's the mestre who can't see a female student in an asexual vein. I would estimate that the majority of mestres are able to treat female capoeiristas with the dignity and respect that they deserve, but there are too many who can't. In the case of this particular female capoeirista, her mestre couldn't see her as just a capoeirista.

Once they started dating, she and her boyfriend, who was a capoeirista in the same group, had the same cord and always came to class together. They both trained with the same frequency and dedication, but their relationships with the mestre were distinctly different. Her boyfriend enjoyed frequent conversations with the mestre, both capoeira-related and personal. She, on the other hand, was not so fortunate. Once she started dating her boyfriend, the mestre stopped talking to her.

She kept track of her interactions with the mestre, and for more than a year the mestre said hello to her only when she greeted him upon arrival at class, and goodbye to her when she spoke to him upon leaving. He never made corrections in her game, shared his wisdom in the art form, or complimented her for anything she did right. It was as if she were invisible. Because she wasn't available romantically, she wasn't worth his time. Instead of nurturing her natural abilities as a capoeirista, he completely disregarded her as a person. She had to find her worth as a capoeirista, and improve her skills, without the help of her mestre, who should have been cultivating her self-esteem and skill but was in fact inhibiting it, or at best neglecting it.

I have trained and played with many a capoeirista, both in the United States and Brazil, and regardless of where I go, I see students subjected to unnecessary abuse. The common thread found in each occasion regardless of group, style, and culture is the student's love for capoeira and their group, which keeps them holding on to a situation that is unhealthy—much like a man or woman fighting to stay in a bad romantic relationship.

I believe there are some fundamental characteristics required to be a teacher. Often I am asked by friends for referral to a capoeira instructor in whatever city they live in. If I know of someone I feel comfortable with, I will pass on this name or names, but if I don't personally know of a particular teacher in that area, I advise the friend to look for certain characteristics— namely competence, respect for students, integrity, temperance, humility, and a nurturance of students' development.

Some of these traits may not be detectable the first time you visit a class. On the other hand, some characteristics of a teacher are easily detected in the first class or two. Arrogance and an ill temper generally show themselves early in your interaction with a teacher. When you see these red flags, take note and act accordingly.

Below is a more detailed discussion of characteristics you should look for when evaluating a teacher.

# Competence

The proliferation of capoeira classes in the United States is evident—capoeira's popularity has exploded over the past fifteen years, and there is a huge demand for classes. Capoeira is offered in fitness gyms, after-school programs, and cultural centers throughout the country. Unfortunately, this has provided an opening for charlatans with little to no legitimate preparation as a teacher to pass themselves off as bonafide instructors. There are far too many individuals whom I categorize as "Internet capoeiristas"—they go online to learn as much as they can about capoeira, then they begin calling themselves capoeiristas and instructors without any formal training under a qualified teacher.

Capoeira is about a lifestyle. To be qualified to teach capoeira, you need to have learned the history, culture, and context of the movements from someone qualified to teach them. An old kung fu *sifu* (master) once told me that you can't become a master without receiving master knowledge. Put another way, your teacher can only teach you what they know. If a "teacher" only knows physical movements, he can only teach you physical movements, and you will learn only physical movements. This starts you down the path of becoming a break dancer or a gymnast. Both have movements in common with capoeira, but they are not capoeira.

Additionally, physical talent alone doesn't qualify someone to be a teacher. Capoeira is a way of thinking. If you recall from the section on "The Roda," I talked about capoeira being mostly mental, and the physical aspect being secondary. I have seen too many individuals with athletic talent prop themselves up as teachers, yet they lack a deeper understanding of capoeira and the rich lessons that the art form has to offer about the *roda* and life. How can this person guide others along their path as a capoeirista?

# Respect

This is simple. A teacher must have respect for his students, and the students must have respect for their teacher. If you find yourself in a class where either of these is lacking, this is probably not an environment you want to train in. You deserve and need your teacher to respect you. If you see that a teacher lacks respect for his students, then you are setting yourself up for abuse and/or conflict. Additionally, if the students don't respect the teacher, then this says something about the manner in which the teacher conducts himself. If a teacher doesn't command respect through his or her conduct, I repeat, what can they teach you?

# Integrity

The concept of integrity is far too under-emphasized in capoeira but is nonetheless necessary in a qualified teacher. If a teacher does not have integrity, then there can be no trust. If a student can't trust his teacher, then the teacher can't pass on knowledge to the student. How can you believe anything that someone says when you believe that person to lack integrity? Going back to the previous story of the woman who quit capoeira never wanting to have anything to do with it again: her mestre had lost all integrity in her eyes, and nothing he did or said held credibility for her. Unfortunately, she transferred all of what she felt for him onto all of capoeira and abandoned the art. The effect was unfortunate, but it's a natural progression if your mestre lacks integrity.

# Temperance

All emotions should be held in due bounds. Anger is okay, but not unchecked anger. Becoming frustrated is okay, but that frustration should not be allowed to run rampant. This is true for anyone, and as a teacher of others, you have to exemplify this for your students.

A teacher should not be emotionless. Having human emotions plays a big role in being a qualified teacher, but being able to temper those emotions is crucial. When an impulse arises, a teacher should be able to weigh the consequences of the action(s) inspired by that impulse, and then proceed with discretion and fairness. An individual incapable of tempering his emotions is not someone you should ever make yourself subject to on any level.

I have had students who frustrated and annoyed me. I have had students who flat-out angered me. One such student was a blue cord who angered me to such a degree, I had the impulse to take him into the *roda* and kick him as hard as I could. Though I could have "justified" my actions, I knew it wouldn't have been the right thing to do. My kicking him wouldn't have improved the situation on any level. I would have let my impulses rule my judgment, and the end result would have been a deteriorated situation. Through temperance, and a long-distance phone call to Brazil for some input from my mestre, I was able to address the situation appropriately, which in turn made me a better teacher and my student a better student.

# Humility

Teachers must be humble. I once heard the saying that a wise man knows that he knows nothing at all. Though it is true that teachers have a great deal of information about capoeira, in the grand scheme of things what they know is only a sentence in the universe's book of knowledge. Even if you restrict it to capoeira, think of all that has happened in the history of this amazing art form. Think of all the mestres. Think of all the *rodas*. Think of all the songs that have been written and sung. What any one teacher of capoeira can know of such a vast history is only a minute fraction of what has occurred. You should be leery of any teacher who thinks he is the end-all, be-all of capoeira. In order to cultivate a student, a teacher must remember what it is like to be a novice, and from an empathetic place interact with the student.

# Nurturing

In capoeira, as in anything, you are starting from point A and you're trying to progress to points B, C, D, and so on. Teachers must invest time, energy, and knowledge into their students. Your development as a capoeirista isn't much different than your development from a child to an adult. At different stages you need distinctly different things. Like babies need shelter and protection, so does a novice capoeirista; like an adolescent needs to learn responsibility and accountability, so does an intermediate student developing into a graduated student; like an adult needs the necessary skills to live independently and be productive, so does a beginning instructor starting out on the path to becoming a mestre. Whoever your teacher is, he or she needs to be willing and able to guide through all of these stages.

# 8

# Capoeira: Brazil vs. USA

More than anything else, whether it's here or when I'm traveling in Brazil, I am frequently asked how capoeira in the U.S. compares to capoeira in Brazil. The general assumption is that there is a major gap in capoeira quality between the two countries. This assumption is both true and false.

Capoeira is huge in Brazil. It's everywhere down there. I remember the first time I traveled to Salvador, Bahia; I was struck by the pay phones on the street shaped like *berimbaus*. Capoeira is a major part of Brazilian culture, so not expecting a difference would be silly. A majority of Brazilians train capoeira at some point in their lives, and whether they have trained capoeira or not, everyone knows exactly what capoeira is. The number of mestres in all the United States might equal the number of mestres you can find in a mid-sized city in Brazil.

I compare capoeira in Brazil to basketball in the U.S. Basketball is played globally, but the level of basketball played in the States is far superior to that of the rest of the world. Kids here grow up playing basketball as soon as they can walk, their heroes are basketball players, and the level of competition is high. As a result, they develop into amazing basketball players. That's how it is in Brazil with respect to capoeira. Everywhere you go in Brazil you see a capoeirista with amazing talent, and it's this large talent pool that raises the competitive bar constantly, which in turn raises the level of capoeira.

But don't discredit capoeira in the Northern Hemisphere just yet. To use the basketball analogy again, Americans are the best at it in general, but you have great basketball players from Germany, France, Brazil, and several other countries. The same can be said for capoeira. Brazil is where it's at, but capoeira has spread all over the world and there are great capoeiristas everywhere. I have played with capoeiristas from all over the world who are as proficient as their Brazilian counterparts. I have seen a whole generation develop in the United States that makes me very optimistic about the growing tradition of capoeira here. For every great *graduado* (graduated student whose level is indicated by the color of cord/belt that he wears) that you have coming up in Brazil, there is a "Chegado," "Muito Tempo," "Pente," or "Manteiga" in the U.S.; for every great instructor or professor in Brazil, there is a "Xango," "Cangaceiro," "Enyoka," or "Malandro." By the way, these nicknames are common in capoeira and indicate a personal characteristic about each individual, oftentimes poking fun at the capoeirista. I arrived late to a class one day so I was given the nickname "Tartaruga" or "Turtle." There was an added level of teasing in the nickname because I liked to play capoeira fast, so the association with being slow wasn't a good thing.

There are increasingly more serious, dedicated, and talented

Cangaceiro and Siamesa

capoeiristas coming along each day in the U.S. In general, this is how I would characterize the differences between capoeira in Brazil and the United States:

# Brazil

*Music:* In Brazil almost everyone is a musician. One of the most amazing things I have ever seen was on my first trip there. After the *batizado* of Professor Zezinho, we all went to a pool party at the home of one of the students. There was top-of-the-line stereo equipment in the pool house, but instead of turning on the CD player, people pulled out *timbãos*, *pandeiros*, *atabaques*, and whatever else they could find to beat on, and they had an impromptu concert right there poolside that lasted for more than an hour. These weren't professional musicians; they were just everyday folks. With such a rich musical culture, you can imagine how that affects the music in capoeira. This ability can really be seen in *Maculelê* (warrior stick dance associated with capoeira). The level of drumming that is standard in Brazil is really high.

Also, when it comes to singing, all capoeira songs are in Portuguese, so obviously learning and writing new songs is exponentially easier for Brazilians. I have seen new capoeira songs composed by Brazilians in five minutes while we're driving down the street. Since they are writing songs in their native language, metaphor and symbolism are easily infused into their lyrics. It reminds me of my U.S. friends who are rappers and can write an entire rap song in a matter of minutes.

*Physical Game:* The quality of capoeira in general is pretty high in Brazil. This makes sense given that capoeira has evolved in Brazil for more than four hundred years. Everywhere you look there are amazing mestres who are world-renowned. If you take a city like Rio de Janeiro, São Paulo, or Salvador, I wouldn't be able to give you a comprehensive list of all the mestres in any of these particular cities. There are just too many to know them all. Whenever I travel to Salvador, I feel like I miss out because even if I am there for two weeks, I can't see all the mestres that I would like to. If I go train with Mestre René, then I miss the opportunity to train with Mestre Nenel. If I take a trip out to Mestre Duende's class, then I will miss the *roda* at Mestre João Pequeno's. Then there are all the mestres that I know of but have never had the opportunity to train with—Mestres Sombra, Valmir, Bamba, etc. With access to such a body of knowledge, the technical precision in Brazil is remarkable.

Brazilians also play capoeira with a lot more intensity on average. Because the talent level of capoeiristas in Brazil is so high, when they play each other they constantly have to take their games to the next level. In my group (Raízes do Brasil), which isn't unique in this way, there is a cadre of amazing *professores* and *contramestres* who will be the next generation of mestres. When they all come together to play, the intensity of the *roda* is overwhelming. Often when I take my students to Brazil and they see these guys play capoeira, it's almost too much for them to take in. In any sport/athletic event, you can only become the best you can be by competing against the best. In Brazil, the best players train and play together every day, and consequently their games are always rising to new heights.

There is another element present in Brazil that raises the bar: capoeiristas are more aggressive. Two capoeiristas pushing their games to the brink of a fight in Brazil is common. When this happens the *roda* continues as if it's no big deal. Knowing this, capoeiristas come to class with a heightened level of intensity, and the games that result are considered normal.

Among the people who know what capoeira is in the U.S., the biggest misconception is that capoeira is more of a dance than a martial art, and that there isn't any contact. They think this because their exposure to capoeira has been limited and they probably have only seen demonstrations. There is contact in capoeira, and in Brazil it's common for one capoeirista to kick another—often with a lot of force—and then after the roda those two capoeiristas act as if nothing happened.

*History:* To my surprise, the average student of capoeira in Brazil isn't as versed in the history of capoeira as I expected. At first this puzzled me, but after having traveled to Brazil several times and met quite a few capoeiristas, I came to understand why. The history of capoeira isn't stagnant. It is constantly expanding, and new chapters are being written by the countless great contemporary capoeiristas. Because of this, many up-and-coming capoeiristas in Brazil have only general knowledge about the traditional history of capoeira because they are extremely knowledgeable about the history of their own mestre, and the mestres who had a direct effect on their capoeira education.

I once had a conversation with a *contramestre* in our school, and he admitted that he knew only core aspects of the history of Mestre Bimba; he didn't know all the particulars. He went on to explain that though he didn't know every in and out of Mestre Bimba's life, he could tell you anything you wanted to know about Mestre Ralil and Mestre Edinho. The lives of these two mestres were much more relevant to his development in capoeira, so as a result their histories in capoeira were what he studied more intensely. If as a capoeirista you have the privilege of learning from Mestres Suasuna, Moraes, Mão Branca, or Curió, you are going to acquire a lot more information about these mestres than you would about Mestres Caiçara, Noronha, or Traira, who have already passed on to the realm of the ancestors.

# The United States of America

*Music:* American capoeiristas start out learning music in capoeira very dogmatically. Most times they have never seen a *berimbau* or heard Portuguese before they took their first capoeira class. Because of this, they don't learn capoeira music as intuitively as Brazilians do. For instance, when teaching American students to play the *berimbau*, I find that each rhythm has to be broken down step by step and note by note. This is how Americans play the *berimbau* in the beginning. You can hear them counting the notes in their head as they play.

It's the same when learning how to play the *atabaque* for *Maculelê*, or the *pandeiro* for *Samba de Roda*. American capoeiristas generally take longer to learn how to naturally play these instruments with swing and *tempero* (spice). With me being more of a purist when it comes to the *bateria*, I have come to appreciate the benefit of Americans learning how to play the instruments in this manner. They acquire an in-depth understanding of how the *berimbau* layers over the baseline 1-2-3 rhythm of the *roda*, and as a result those who become proficient *berimbau* players learn how to generate an amazing amount of *axé* (energy) in the *roda*. Each instrument has a particular role, and because Americans learn how to play the instruments by the steps, they tend to conform to these traditional expectations.

When it comes to the Portuguese-language songs of capoeira, Americans are definitely disadvantaged. When you step into your first *roda* as an American, you have no idea what the lyrics of the songs mean. I remember as a raw cord I was swept—my feet came up above my head, or at least it felt that way—and someone sang the lyrics *"Mais um facão bateu embaixo, a bananeiro caiu...."* This translates to "From one more low blow from the machete, the banana tree fell." Everyone was laughing and smiling, but the message went entirely over my head.

One question that Brazilians always ask me is whether Americans sing songs in English in the *roda*. The answer is no. The way Americans go about learning capoeira lyrics is formulaic. They get a copy of the song written in Portuguese with the English translation written alongside so that they have an idea what they are singing. From there they commit the lyrics to memory in Portuguese. Obviously this takes longer, but the chain effect of this learning process is that American capoeiristas sing more traditional capoeira songs than do Brazilians. This is because Brazilians are always writing new music. I haven't been to Brazil for a year, so the "new" songs that I learned last year are old by now. There have been at least thirty new songs composed and introduced as regular songs into the *roda* in my school since I was last there.

*Physical Game:* Americans have made great strides in the past few years in the quality of their capoeira games. Ten years ago, there was a huge disparity in the skill level of an orange cord, an intermediate student, in Brazil and an orange cord in the U.S. (By the way, the color sequence for cords is white, yellow, orange, blue [first graduate cord], green, purple, brown, red [mestre]. This is my school's cord system and it's one of the two popular cord systems. The other is based on the colors of the Brazilian flag.) This disparity was due to the fact that the history of capoeira here was a decade less developed than it is now, and the number of capoeiristas was much smaller. But in the last ten years, the number of mestres who have moved to the States from Brazil has increased, the number of capoeiristas has increased, and capoeira has gained more notoriety in the States. Because of this, all kinds of people from all kinds of backgrounds are being attracted to capoeira. Specifically, more kids and teenagers have taken up capoeira, and because of their young age they have a tremendous advantage. Also, capoeira has now become more accepted as a valid martial art, so there are more capoeiristas in the U.S. who train and play with a higher level of intensity than formerly.

The growth of capoeira has done wonders for the credibility of American capoeiristas. There are now American orange, blue, and green cords who play capoeira just as well as any orange, blue, and green cords in Brazil.

One distinct difference between the games in the two countries is the level of intensity. Each year there are more and more proficient American capoeiristas, but Americans don't challenge each other as much as capoeiristas do in Brazil. Let me be clear: American capoeiristas challenge each other. It just doesn't happen as often as it does in Brazil. This is because a hard game is taken a lot more personally by Americans than it is by Brazilians. This is a cultural difference, and I'm curious to see how it plays out in the development of capoeira in the States. I say this because in capoeira we don't wear any padding or protective equipment, so when someone gets kicked, it is a very personal

Pintado

matter. As a result, a *ponteira* to the stomach today is going to have a lingering effect for months and maybe years later in the mind of an American capoeirista.

Another major difference in the games in the two countries involves female capoeiristas. Interestingly enough, it has been my experience that female capoeiristas in the States play at a higher level than they do in Brazil. I believe this has to do with the difference in the respective cultures. The social expectations of women in Brazil and the U.S. differ quite a bit, and because of this American women are able to commit more time to their training. There are plenty of amazing women capoeiristas in Brazil. To name a few that I know, there is Professora Ruli from Raízes do Brasil, Chris from ACANNE (Associação de Capoeira Angola Navio Negreiro) and Contramestre Janja from Nzinga.

But once women in Brazil start families, it becomes extremely difficult if not impossible for them to continue a consistent training regimen. In the States this is less of an issue.

*History:* Because capoeira isn't as abundant here in the U.S. as it is in Brazil, American capoeiristas seek out as much information as possible about the history of capoeira. It's not common knowledge here that enslaved Africans created capoeira. It's not common knowledge that such a thing as capoeira even exists. So when American students get involved in capoeira, they want to learn as much as they possibly can about the art form. And to do this, they draw on as many sources of knowledge as possible.

I remember when I first started capoeira, I would go to the computer lab on campus with the intention of writing my history paper. I would tell myself that I was just going to look at a couple of capoeira websites, and before I knew it, I had spent more than two hours sifting through the content of as many websites as I could find in English. Because we Americans aren't surrounded by capoeira, students learn everything they can about it in order to strengthen their connection to it.

# 9

# A Few U.S. Capoeiristas: In Their Own Words

Capoeira and the capoeira community have been international for decades. Consequently there many capoeiristas who aren't Brazilian but live capoeira as authentically as their Brazilian counterparts. What distinguishes these capoeiristas from those in Brazil is their world view. Throughout this book I have been sharing my unique perspective as one representative voice of a non-Brazilian capoeira teacher. In this chapter I include two interviews I conducted, along with a short essay, representing three capoeiristas from the United States who have perspectives representative of many other capoeiristas.

The first interview is with "Rolo," a former capoeirista who left the art form due to cultural differences. The second interview is with "Kevin," a veteran capoeirista who built a capoeira school in Madison, Wisconsin, where capoeira was completely unknown. The short essay is written by "Girasol," an up-and-coming female capoeirista.

## Rolo

■ *Why did you start training capoeira?*

I liked the music and I knew that it had African origins. I had a previous martial arts background, which was more or less the martial aspect of fighting. There was something very appealing about people actually moving to the music inside a *roda,* dancing with each other, and responding to each other, and I thought that it would be something challenging to me because I am not necessarily a big dancer. So I decided that I actually wanted to participate in this African art.

■ *How would you compare capoeira to other martial arts that you have a background in?*

I would say that capoeira has a martial arts aspect, but it's not so much that you are actually fighting the other person and there is clashing and friction. It's literally moving in harmony with the person, which actually takes more skill because you have to respond to the other individual; whereas I found in other martial arts that I don't necessarily have to respond to the other individual. I can just throw a punch and hit them or kick them—you know, maybe block an attempted attack and throw a punch or a kick. In capoeira that's not the case. You literally have to flow with the kick or whatever is coming towards you and respond in a harmonious way. I found that more challenging and actually more in harmony with universal principles. I found it spiritual, as a matter of fact. I would say that capoeira is more spiritual than my exposure to more traditional martial arts.

■ *Okay. So running with that theme as a martial artist, what do you consider to be capoeira's greatest attribute or attributes?*

I think playing in the *roda* would be the biggest [attribute]. It sums up all of capoeira to me because you have to move to the music while also moving to your partner in a call-and-response way. I just think that the overall concept of playing in the *roda* is the biggest thing because it's not an easy thing. In order to play in the *roda* you must spend time to learn to become a singer, to play a particular instrument.... I think that helps you become a better player in the *roda* so it's a cumulative thing. So I would say playing in the *roda* is the biggest attribute. It's just a wonderful thing to reach that point.

■ *This is kind of an open-ended question. When you look at capoeira from your viewpoint, how do you see it?*

I think the art of itself is a beautiful thing. But I think a lot of the individuals.... In the question there are two things: there is the concept of capoeira, and then there is the practical application of capoeira—what people are actually doing. And I think the concept of capoeira is beautiful. I have found from my experiences that people who play what is considered Angola capoeira are closer to that ideal. I find that with the Regional capoeira—although you have some very good people that you see at certain functions and actually want to play with—the spiritual concept seems to be lost. There is a lot of friction and conflict going on, and I think that takes away from the beauty of the art. People begin to fight and turn it into something ugly, which even violates the rules of capoeira itself and how it's actually taught. I have to separate the concept of capoeira from how it's actually practiced by individuals who tend to bring in the element of machismo, which violates the principles or the spiritual context of capoeira.

■ *Do you think there are oppressive forces within capoeira? And if so, what are they?*

I do believe there are oppressive forces, but these forces, I would say, are brought into capoeira by people, and it's not actually in the art itself. One example is trying to control individuals because there is this competition between the schools to get really great practitioners of the art who will thereby promote a particular teacher. At functions where many schools are present, maybe a particular student doesn't shine as well as a student from another school. Maybe it's an unwritten rule that when you are shown up in the *roda*, you begin a fight, because it seems like that is ingrained in students from all schools. Instead of saying that maybe I need to go practice more so that I can be in more harmony—maybe dance with this individual—students have been trained to fight in the name of the instructor, not necessarily because that student feels that he has to fight. It's just that they have been conditioned to do so.

Also, I don't know if it's just built into the Brazilian culture, but I also find that capoeira is oppressive towards women. When the art is considered a spiritual thing—it's a dance, being able to flow with the other person—I found that men didn't necessarily like to play with women because maybe the game could not be tough enough. And so it tended to be women playing with women as opposed to it being a mixture of men and women playing. So in the sense of it being a spiritual art, I think women receive less of it only because they are not necessarily allowed to fully participate because of what I consider this chauvinistic aspect. And I don't know if it's in the art because it has always been there since its inception, or if it's in the art because the people who are now the guardians of the art have decided to be chauvinistic.

■ *Do you think capoeira can empower its practitioners? And if so, how?*

[Laughter] It definitely can empower its practitioners! It empowered me! I was a person not willing to sing because I am not the best of singers, a person who does not dance, a person, outside of Spanish, who has never really tried to learn a foreign language, and the fact is that you have to participate in this art, you have to sing, you have to develop rhythm, you have to sing in Portuguese (which is a beautiful thing and you find out that you are actually learning a language while playing).... The journey—I'm not an instrument player either—the journey to building your own instrument (because that's what is built into capoeira, you have to build your own berimbaus) to learning to play an instrument and being in rhythm and singing at the same time—oh, it's definitely empowering! Especially since you're in a group where many people have been in the same position. It's not like everyone in there is a great singer, etc. So when you're attempting to sing and you're not necessarily hitting all the notes, it's really not a big deal. People understand as long as the energy is appropriate. And eventually it gives you time to get your voice together, get your rhythm together. So it empowers people, I think, to do things they have never done before.

But also it's empowering when you play in the *roda*. I found that my background in terms of martial arts helped me (I've sparred before), but for people who have been shy, who are not confrontational in the sense of being in a struggle, to actually come into the *roda* and to move in harmony with another person while throwing kicks and responding—I think it empowers those shy individuals to tap into something that's actually bigger than themselves and do something outside their comfort zone. So it is really empowering and I think it's a beautiful thing. You see that all people, regardless of background, will learn something and be pushed to do something that you are not comfortable doing, but it's in an environment where it's acceptable. Oh, it's a beautiful thing!

- *With all that being said, is there anything else you would like to say about your experience in capoeira, or about the art in general?*

For capoeira here in the United States, and abroad, I think that if it wants to continue to flourish and thrive, that the people who are the guardians, the mestres, the schools out there, actually need to take their own personal beliefs to a level that's more inclusive. I know there is competition in the art itself, but when it breaks down and turns into physical fights and confrontations, it takes something that is beautiful and turns it into not necessarily an art, but something in which people might not want to participate.

One of the reasons that I stopped participating in the art is because of the fighting. I actually have a background in martial arts where fighting takes place, but at my age when I entered into capoeira—I was in my thirties—I was a married man with children, and I got into a fight with a nineteen-year-old kid. I was able to execute a move and then this kid was actually taught that if a person with a lower belt executes a move on you, then you need to defend your higher ranking by getting into a fight. And so the young kid actually tried to fight me, but unlike other people I was not somebody who was new to fighting. It was self-defense because the kid was actually punching me and even bit me. And I thought that something like that was totally ridiculous. We were classmates. We were from the same school and it was in class. And I thought that was pretty ridiculous for a grown man who was married with two children to be at his own school and to get into a fight with one of his classmates because the instructor had taught revenge. That really bothered me.

Then going to other schools and seeing beautiful art being demonstrated, I saw the same thing: when one school's practitioner is able to execute a move on another, things degenerate to fights, and then mestres actually condone it. That's not healthy. That's not good because most of the people I saw practicing the art were adults. That was the only thing that I really liked about traditional martial arts; when you did have a sparring competition or what you technically would call a fight, it was literally just a competition. When it was over, whether you won or lost, there weren't any hard feelings between the two combatants. But in capoeira that's not the case. Fights become real. There is real emotion. There is real anger. And that's not good—especially for adults to be tapping into that, and actually applying that anger towards another person.

To this day that is why I do not practice the art. I know that if you go someplace—and as a capoeirista you want to go to other schools, you want to see other people play and their different styles of play, you want to see the best—there is always going to be an altercation. I just don't have time for that as a grown man. I think it's embarrassing for the art itself.

## Kevin

■ *How did you get introduced to capoeira?*

The first reference that I ever saw to it was in a movie called *Rooftops,* which was in the early eighties, I guess, and there was some sort of what they called combat dance, which was a blend of break dancing and capoeira kicks. I saw somebody do *passagem* (a counter movement to get behind your opponent) and an *armada* and I was like "I don't know what that is, but I gotta learn how to do it!" That was it, you know. It had everything I was interested in: martial arts, acrobatics, music, flair, style.

■ *What do you get out of coming to capoeira class day in and day out?*

Besides the physical release, the intense concentration on what you're doing on your hands, your feet, your contact with the ground, your opponent.... It takes you out of your everyday life. It takes you out of the things that seem important and it puts you in sort of a survival mode, I guess—more of a primal mode.

■ *How would you assess capoeira in the United States?*

It's gaining notoriety, it's gaining popularity, but at the same time, being that there is no standard of measure, it's not codified, there are no accredited federations, so capoeira is maybe not represented as well as it could be. While on the whole it's good because more people are starting to hear about and become familiar with it, I guess I would worry a little about the integrity of the way the art is being presented. It's sort of being over-commercialized for foreign markets.

■ *Considering the commercialization that has crept into capoeira in the United States, what are the major differences that you see in capoeira here and in Brazil?*

You could say that in Brazil it is much more of an organic art form. Capoeira sort of springs up naturally. It doesn't just happen in the academy, in the classes, in the structured environments; it happens between friends on an informal level—people playing music, and playing and practicing [capoeira], and showing off, and innovating. Whereas here in the States, it hasn't hit that level yet. It's still really taking place only in a very controlled situation. It's like you have basketball, and now you have street hoops and the whole street hoops movement, which is taking ball handling and everything else to a new level. It's the same thing: Maybe after a while when capoeira transcends to that next level, when it becomes more ingrained and more people are growing up familiar with it, and it starts to happen more spontaneously like that, then I think you will start to see a little bit more integrity. You will see more natural ability, and I think that naturally leads to building organization.

■ *In capoeira in general, here in the United States or abroad, is there anything you would like to see changed about it or represented more? And if so, what?*

This is coming from my own bias, but when I found capoeira and where I started, there was almost no one so anyone who did capoeira was welcomed and embraced regardless of whether it was slightly different or maybe even contrasting in style. And I think it seems that now as part of the evolution, people are struggling for their own identity in an art that is sort of nascent and growing, so there is too much insecurity to interact with people and embrace the differences that others are emphasizing. I would say that it is really unfortunate that there isn't more interaction between schools and styles.

## Girasol

As with any relationship, my engagement with capoeira has been a dynamic one in constant ebb and flow. The complexity of a capoeirista's relationship to capoeira will largely depend on the level of commitment to the art. From an aesthetic point of view, capoeira appears mesmerizing, and combined with music it can even be hypnotic. Without a doubt many people are drawn to it for these reasons.

For me, capoeira's aesthetic value cannot be disentangled from its cultural value. Capoeira's cultural value is composed of many socio-historical elements, including capoeira's controversial and contested origins.

Capoeira's history up until the mid-twentieth century has been one dominated and shaped by men. When capoeira hit the scene in the U.S. during the 1970s, women were quick to break the gender divide that may have prevailed in Brazil. For me history is important, and capoeira's songs provide a vast tapestry of oral tradition. I know of no songs that immortalize a woman for her capoeira abilities. Nowadays the number of women playing capoeira tends to be equal to that of men, and there are even a few women mestres. The existence of women capoeira teachers is important for the status of all women training capoeira.

Luckily the group I train with works hard to maintain the balance that capoeira represents and needs—this has largely shaped my experience with capoeira. Although women are absent from most of capoeira's history, there is now a space for us, but this space had to be negotiated, and sometimes still has to be. For example, when I was training in Oakland with my teacher Tartaruga, at one point the group dynamic shifted when a few strong women capoeiristas could not train as much as they used to, and therefore women had less of a presence. The shift could be felt in the overly aggressive energy that began to surround the games in the *roda*. After a few weeks of this, and discussions with some of the other women in the group, I initiated a conversation with Tartaruga about it. In order for me to feel comfortable as a woman playing capoeira, aggressive energy has to be regulated. I don't know what he said or did, but things were under control after our conversation. This is one type of negotiation I am describing.

Men are not the only ones who can be overly aggressive, as my experience visiting Brazil demonstrated. Mestre Papiba, a mestre in our group who teaches in California but is from Brazil, has often said that Brazilians fight more whereas Americans talk more. This also applies to female Brazilian capoeiristas. When I visited Brazil I was amazed at how hostile a lot of the women's play was in the women's *rodas*. That's another thing—women were often shut out of the *roda* by the men, so we would form our own. In one of these all-women *rodas* real violence erupted one evening. Knowing my own comfort zone, I only played a little that night and with good cause. A young woman injured her wrist from being repeatedly taken down. She was wearing a brace the following day. Eventually the mestres had to intervene because the violence had escalated to a dangerous level. So I admit that women can be just as violent and aggressive as men, but from my experience it is usually the men who play with a higher level of aggression.

In the United States I have had the experience of participating in a few all-women *rodas* that were organized by three graduated women capoeiristas from different groups. The intentions behind this monthly event were auspicious. These women felt, as did I, that this type of event could help bridge the politics that prevent healthy interactions between groups. One of the organizers was from our group, and the initial *roda* was totally inspiring. Some of the best female capoeiristas from the [San Francisco] Bay Area were at this first *roda*, and the energy was positive throughout the entire event. Unfortunately, the women's monthly *roda* lost its momentum after the first event and never quite regained that initial level.

Although it only lasted for a few months, it was always empowering to witness a *roda* completely sustained by women. During a normal [both sexes] *roda* it is not uncommon for women to take the background in regard to playing music, singing, and even playing in the *roda*. With the all-women *roda* we were forced to rely on ourselves, and seeing other women proficient in the many intricacies of the art of capoeira made a lasting impression.

My overall experience in capoeira has been one of positivity and empowerment. Being a woman capoeirista challenges stereotypes that define women as weak and fragile, or as needing protection from men. Historically capoeira has been dominated my men, though nowadays women are helping to create a place in capoeira's history for women. We will continue to be an integral part of capoeira's healthy existence now and in the future.

# 10

# *Nosso Quilombo*

My journey as a capoeira teacher has been rewarding on so many levels. The primary benefit of my teaching career has been the relationships I have cultivated and the lives I have been able to impact. I have met and come to know people from so many different walks of life. I've had the opportunity to work with so many amazing young people, helping them grow into the adults they wanted to be. Capoeira, with all its many benefits, offered me a valuable toolset and a new world to introduce to my students, which in turn empowered them to make a new world for themselves.

On September 1, 1998, I taught my first capoeira class for children in east Oakland at the Rainbow Recreation Center. I had a *berimbau* that I made myself and a crappy *pandeiro* that I purchased on Haight Street in San Francisco. And without a penny of funding, I embarked on a journey that was more enriching then I could have ever imagined.

I had been living in the Bay Area for a few years and could have opened a class pretty much anywhere. East Oakland is where I considered home (in the Bay Area) since that's where I lived when I first arrived from Los Angeles, and I have family that have lived in Oakland for generations. I worked and attended school in San Francisco, and I lived in Berkeley right next to the university. I easily could have started a class in either one of these cities, but because of the years I spent visiting east Oakland as a teenager, and the subsequent years I spent there as a resident, I knew that I didn't want to do my work in any other community. There was a genuine need there for an uplifting force in the midst of depressing circumstances, and I related to this. I had grown up in the same environment, just in another zip code. I knew firsthand what lay in wait for the youth of east Oakland if they didn't find another path—death and oppression. I also knew that if given the resources or simply an honest chance to succeed, many of these youth could reach extreme heights.

When I first started teaching I knew that I had to be there for the long haul to have a genuine effect. All too often you have poverty pimps that arrive from wherever, and they'll do a mural, or run a short-term program, then they'll leave and feel that they "invested" in the community. I remember once talking with a student of mine about this phenomenon and explaining why I had decided to run the program year-round, only taking a break for a week or two around Christmas. I explained that these youth lived amongst misery all day, every day, 365 days a year, and if we wanted to have a real impact on their lives we needed to create an alternate reality for these youth to live in. There needed to be a separate community that they could be a part of—a community with its own norms, culture, and expectations separate from those of the community in which they currently resided. A community where excelling in school was not only okay but expected. Staying free from drug use was demanded. Involvement in gangs was unnecessary. Though there is no slave plantation in east Oakland and no one is owned from birth by another man—individuals are free to come and go as they please—the oppressive forces working against these young people are just as real. Because of this I wanted to establish a community free from oppression. I wanted to establish a *quilombo—Nosso Quilombo!* A *quilombo* was a community established in the jungle or mountains of Brazil by runaway slaves. Here they were able to live freely according to their traditional values and customs. *Nosso* means "our." I used the term *"Nosso Quilombo"* to conceptualize for my students that we were establishing our own community free from the ills that plagued the larger community we lived in. To reach this goal, I felt that capoeira was the perfect instrument to work with. The flash of the kicks, the awesomeness of the flips, and the intoxication of the pulsating rhythm produced by the *bateria* are perfect for catching the attention of youngsters. Beyond that, the constant reminder of inequality and the ability to address inequality that capoeira offers is invaluable. So in the waning days of the summer of 1998, I began trying to convince east Oakland youth to run for the hills and rise above the drugs, gangs, and pervasive culture of death that hovered above and around them.

It was routine to experience extreme violence, often in broad daylight, in and around Rainbow Recreation Center—the neighborhood park where I taught for the first five years. I once had to enter a circle of fifteen or so youth and adults that had gathered around to watch five other kids jump one of my students. It was clear that some of the people in the circle wanted to assault me for breaking up the fight. Another incident involved an older gentleman being knocked unconscious and robbed right outside my class window.

I can recount numerous tales about the violence in this community, but the most alarming one took place in the middle of summer, 2001. I had dismissed the kids' class, and the adult class was going to begin shortly. Because it was around 6:30 PM, the park was still full of playing children, including most of my kids' class. Out of nowhere it seemed, shots rang out, sending the park into chaos. I was inside the classroom and thought of all the kids outside in harm's way. I yelled for everyone who had arrived for the adult class to get down, then I ran to try and round up all of the kids outside. As I made it to the door, my student Cachoeira, who was coming back from the corner store, came dashing toward me with a group of my students. We brought those kids inside and went back to see if anyone else was left outside. Fortunately, the shooter(s) had sped off and no one in the park was harmed.

Beyond this violence, there was the pervasive culture of drug use, drug selling, prostitution, and robbery in the community. I don't want to paint the picture that the majority of the people were like this, because that would not be accurate. What I am saying is the previously mentioned ills were in your face and consistent. So in the midst of this reality, and because of this reality, I taught capoeira. We were Raízes do Brasil Capoeira, but I felt I needed to occasionally refer to our class as *Nosso Quilombo* to orient my students—especially the youth.

My first class was awesome—eleven eager and attentive kids attended. I still remember the looks on their faces: there was

Kevin who stood out as a leader immediately; there was Casey who was so excited by what she was learning that it was hard to keep her in line; there was Keith who was absolutely serious about learning how to fight. There was so much energy in that class on that warm Tuesday afternoon that I didn't know what to do with myself. My brother stopped by to check out the class, and I could see that he was proud of me. When class ended, I reminded the kids that the next class was going to be on Thursday at the same time. That night I was buzzing with excitement. The kids were great—they followed instructions, they were able to do all the movements, and they all said that they were coming to the next class.

My brother gave me some sage advice that turned out to be the greatest advice I've received to date as an instructor: he told me to not get too high with the highs, and not get too low with the lows. When he first told me this I nodded in agreement as a reflex, then he repeated his words. When I heard his advice the second time, it sunk in. He explained that there are going to be high times and low times, and that I needed to remain focused on my greater purpose, regardless of the immediate circumstance. I replay these words of wisdom in my head to this day whenever I'm at either extreme.

As fate would have it, those words rang true much sooner than I expected. The following class there was only one student in attendance—Kevin. I then knew that my mission wasn't going to be a fairy tale. Back down to earth, I taught class just for Kevin. On the surface, the poor attendance seemed to be a setback, but it turned out to be a blessing. The bond created that day between Kevin and me was more beneficial in the establishment of my class than if all eleven students had returned. Kevin was a natural leader and was well respected by the other kids. Along with his obvious commitment, he was unbelievably talented. During that one-on-one class I was able to give him a solid foundation in the basic movements of capoeira, which in turn allowed him to be my model student in subsequent classes. Generally, teachers working in at-risk neighborhoods have to battle to win over that one kid that all the other kids follow, but for many reasons, fate and luck being among them, Kevin was that kid and he willingly stepped up to be a role model.

I continued teaching. Each class there would be one or two new students. A buzz began around the park about the new class. One day when I was walking out to my car to leave, I saw a kid doing a back flip off this huge log in the park. Naturally this caught my attention, and I went up and started talking to him, asking if he had heard of capoeira. He said no. I explained what it was and he was mildly interested, but when I did a back flip for him his eyes opened wide. I asked his name, and he told me it was Bobby. I told him that I expected to see him at the next class. Well, the next class came, and he didn't just show up; he showed up with his sister Jalissa and his brother Anthony. They all wanted to learn how to flip!

Once we got beyond the students' interest in acrobatics, two elements really helped in their development as capoeiristas. One was the seriousness of the neighborhood in which they lived. These kids had known their share of fistfights even at the

Back row: Tre, Casey, Tartaruga, Pintado, Dolphin, Jose, Perna Longa
Front row: Morcego, Tigre, M&M, Sonolento

young ages of ten and eleven, so anything that they learned in the realm of martial arts they took very seriously. They had absolutely no interest in learning how to throw a *martelo* for artistic or aesthetic purposes. All too often I have to appeal to certain adult students to learn the difference between the dance of capoeira and the fight of capoeira. Not with these kids. When they threw an *armada,* they threw it to hit so you'd better *esquiva.*

The second element that served as a great benefit was the size of the room that I taught in. The options for the size of *roda* we could form were small and smaller. Consequently the students had to learn to play capoeira in the proper range. Every *meia-lua-de-compasso* was in range to reach its opponent. This cultivated a genuine dialogue in their games at an extremely early stage. I know graduated students who can't build a fluid dialogue in close range while playing capoeira, yet these nine-, ten-, and eleven-year-old beginner kids were doing so without a second thought.

About four months in, a solid class culture had been set. You were expected to show up to class on time. You were expected to work hard while at class. And most importantly, you were expected to respect yourself, your classmates, and me as the instructor. There were times when I had to dismiss a student from class on a particular day (or even for the next class as well) because they blatantly violated our agreed-upon class rules. Being firm, fair, and consistent, I was able to establish a functional group culture. Kevin (Beaver) was still there training hard; Jalissa (Perna Longa), Anthony (Dolphin), and Bobby (Morcego) were catching up to Kevin rapidly; my nephew Dakare (Tigre) had started training; Casey and Michael were hanging in there even though they weren't learning with the ease of some of the other students; and then there was Yasmin (Pintado), Samuel (Sonolento), Josue (M&M), Yadira, Jose, and Tre. These kids were committed to being capoeiristas one hundred percent.

Classes were held on Tuesdays and Thursdays (later they were expanded to five days a week). Whatever I taught on Tuesday was practiced all day long on Wednesday, and it would show when the students returned to class on Thursday. Whatever was taught on Thursday went through the same process Friday, Saturday, Sunday, and Monday. By the time Tuesday came, the lessons of last Thursday were perfected.

A few months into teaching the class, I left Berkeley and returned to live in my "old neighborhood" in east Oakland only a couple of blocks from the Rec Center. The kids knew this and they would often turn up at my house on Sunday afternoon because they couldn't wait until Tuesday to learn something new. As luck would have it, they always arrived right as I was lying down for a nap. My brother would laugh and tell me to get up. He would remind me what capoeira meant to these kids and that I had a responsibility to them. So there we would be on Sunday afternoon in my front yard holding impromptu capoeira classes. I couldn't give them enough. No matter what I put in front of them, they gobbled it up and were ready for more.

As a reward for their hard work, I began taking the students on trips to play capoeira with other schools. This further solidified our group's bond, and more importantly it opened the kids' eyes up to a world beyond their neighborhood. In fact, it opened my eyes too. I wasn't aware how little these kids knew about the world outside Seminary Avenue and East 14th Street. If I wanted these kids to strive for a world beyond what they saw on a daily basis, then I needed to expose them to that world while providing them some context as to how to interpret it. The only time in my life that I have ever seen someone's breath truly taken away in awe of beauty was when I had Pintado hanging out with me one afternoon. It was a nice day and I wanted to check out the view from the Oakland hills, so I decided to drive along Skyline Boulevard on my way towards north Oakland. As we drove along Skyline we came to a clearing where you could see from the flatlands of east Oakland to downtown Oakland and beyond to downtown San Francisco. It was at this time that Pintado let out a gasp of amazement. I asked him, in surprise, if he had ever been up to the Oakland hills—he lived right down at the base of those same hills. He told me that it was his first time. I knew then that going forward I needed to show these kids as much of the world as I could.

As time went on, I came to learn about the private difficulties the kids were facing as they came to me for advice, support, and intervention. You hear of the horror stories that plague the inner city, but it hits home when there's a ten-year-old face put to it. As I became more aware of the hardships that each kid faced in his or her personal life, I realized that the program needed to be expanded beyond capoeira lessons.

Capoeira had done its job by gaining their attention, and it continued to do its job as a tool of self-discovery and improvement, but there were other aspects of life that needed to be addressed. For instance, puberty came into play as some of the kids got older and new kids joined the class. These youth were bombarded with crude, raw sexuality that if left unchecked would develop unhealthy mentalities. Because of the trust I had earned as their capoeira instructor, I could address these issues. Also, as these kids reached the age of drug experimentation, drug dealing, and gang involvement, my advice didn't fall on deaf ears. My similar upbringing gave me further credibility in their eyes. I was able to serve as a constant reminder that there is another way. Every time they saw me, they saw someone who had "escaped" drugs and alcohol, gangs and prison, and this went a long way in a neighborhood where these destructive elements are pervasive.

In an effort to equip these kids with the some of the tools they needed to rise above the degradation of their community, I started mandatory tutoring sessions to help them with their homework. Also, all the kids were placed on weekly progress reports to monitor their performance in school and ward off any problems before they became crises. We would hold regular discussions dealing with topics ranging from sex, crime, and violence to family, education, and health, and I encouraged an open relationship with the kids' parents to better work together in improving the character of these youngsters. In trying to teach these kids about life, I was always able to refer back to the powerful analogy of struggle and liberation provided by capoeira and its rich history. As a reward for their accomplishments, the kids were taken on trips to San Francisco, the Marin Headlands, Santa Cruz, Los Angeles, and a few as far away as Brazil.

I don't want to give the impression that I did all of this by myself. As the program grew, I had plenty of help. I had also built an adult capoeira class that included working professionals from diverse backgrounds, including teachers, musicians, chefs, business executives, and engineers. These awesome individuals believed in the idea of *Nosso Quilombo* and wanted to invest in it as well. Though they weren't faced with the dangers of being an adolescent in the inner city, they still faced challenges and stress in their lives, and capoeira served as a healthy place for them to escape from their hectic schedules and to rejuvenate their bodies. The adults helped out with tutoring, giving rides home, counseling the kids when necessary, and serving as healthy role models.

Of these amazing individuals, one was truly a godsend. In the summer of 2000, as I was going through a powerful personal transition as a capoeirista, as an instructor, and as a human being, Lisa (Chiclet) joined the *quilombo*. I had just parted ways with my first mestre and was only a blue cord, but I had a group of kids whose lives heavily depended on me as their capoeira teacher, and a group of adults who had bought into the shared vision of the group. Quitting wasn't an option. In order to keep moving the group forward, I was going to need significant assistance.

This is where Chiclet comes into the picture. She had visited other capoeira classes, but when she saw the culture of our class in east Oakland, she knew she wanted to train there. The talents and resources that she brought to the group helped transform our bootstrap little class into a non-profit organization. In class she was my student, but as far as the group was concerned she was my business partner. Our enrollment continued to increase, as well as the breadth and scope of our program. After spending five years housed at the Rainbow Recreation Center, we opened our own studio November 1, 2003. We named it the BAKA Cultural Arts Center. *Baka* is an ancient African word meaning enlightenment and is symbolized by a rising sun. We named the cultural center this because we wanted to expand our offerings beyond capoeira and its related arts, and we felt that our school's name of Raízes do Brasil would define the center as a capoeira school only.

The cultural center housed all our capoeira classes (Raízes do Brasil), as well as our tutoring sessions, performances, workshops, and fundraisers. Beyond that, it served as a resource for the greater community. One of my students, Gina (Bananeira), ran her own youth development program called TEAM, so the cultural center housed them as well. Additionally, there were samba and yoga classes offered for the whole community to participate in.

Over the years a lot of lives were touched through the work I tried to do with capoeira. I believe that capoeira, or any other martial art for that matter, should build character. If not, then there becomes a dangerous imbalance of physical skill and personal accountability. In my years as a capoeira instructor, it has warmed my heart to watch the character of dozens of youth grow and develop, enabling them to be quality young adults. The list includes Segreda, Cabelo, Macaco, Pente, Pimenta, Onda, Camaleão, Pulga, Borrego, Taz, Sonhador, Sorrizinha, Canguru, Dinamite, Montanha, Ursinho, Camarão, Mariposa, and Homem Velho. But beyond these names that I am able to call out off the top of my head, there are so many young people who were a part of the program whose nicknames I can't remember like Thinh-Tai, Rudy, James, Daniel, Casey, and Michael. Each one is a remarkable story, and if given the time and opportunity, I could tell for hours on end how I saw them grow and develop when they stepped within the imaginary borders of our *quilombo*. I am grateful for the opportunity to have worked with each and every one of them. They all have remarkable stories, but I can briefly share only four with you.

**Pintado** started training with my very first group of young students when he was eleven years old, and I am proud to say that he is still a student of mine today. After a few classes I knew that he was going to be a special capoeirista. He demonstrated a creativity that I had never seen in a capoeirista of his age before. It seemed that in each class he had some new move to show me that he had invented, or some new way to combine the moves that I had shown him. He was strong, flexible, and loved to work out. The more I pushed him, the harder he would try. I remember his first class: up to that point every kid in the class had been African-American, and since I had taught the kids that capoeira was invented by African slaves, they didn't think I would let Pintado take class because he was white. I remember that Perna Longa and Dolphin walked up to me and asked, "Can he do capoeira?" I said, "Yes." They quickly responded, "Even though he is white?" I chuckled and reassured them that capoeira is for everyone.

Pintado and his family were Bosnian refugees. They had been placed in a neighborhood that was predominantly African-American, with some Latinos, but definitely a negligible amount of Caucasian people. Pintado was as blond as you could be, and his eyes couldn't have been any bluer. To make him stand out more, he didn't speak English well when I first met him. All this added up to him getting picked on quite a bit at school and around the neighborhood, but he was up to the challenge. He was the third of eight children—all of whom took capoeira with me at some point except for the youngest. His older siblings were twins who, unfortunately, I lost to the streets. Having watched the path that they went down, I was extremely concerned that Pintado was going to follow them.

Pintado didn't really fit anywhere. He had friends, but he was still always different from everyone else in the neighborhood. He dressed like everyone else, he walked like everyone else, he listened to the same music as everyone else, but he looked different and this made him stand out—which in turn led to him getting into a lot of fights. I was always concerned that he was trying too hard to be like everyone else, many of whom were doing the wrong things in life, so I had to pay close attention to his behavior. Sometimes he needed behavior modification.

At home the boy didn't fit in too well, either. His father was very much from the old country, but Pintado had developed a lot of new customs living here in the United States, so this caused them to butt heads. Fortunately, capoeira truly resonated with Pintado, and it provided him an arena to stand out as being great at something. It also provided him an alternative to gangs. I have no doubt that he would have happily followed down the path of his two older brothers if it weren't for capoeira. Feeling like an outsider everywhere he went, Pintado found that our *quilombo* allowed him to be a part of something genuine and fulfilled his need to belong. He rose above his circumstances and now earns a decent and honest living.

**Panteira** was the oldest of three girls living in the Fruitvale District of east Oakland. She is a special soul. When we met she was street smart but still innocent. She was economically disadvantaged but nonetheless brilliant. She wasn't your Hollywood-stereotyped Latina young girl with an attitude problem and a gang-banger boyfriend. She was a straight-A student, honest, and hard-working.

Panteira didn't require much effort on my part in behavior modification, like Pintado. What Panteira needed was a place to simply be a thirteen-year-old. A place where she didn't have to stress about always making the right decision because if she didn't she might ruin her future. Panteira needed a place where she could get help with her essay so that she could keep her 4.0 grade point average, and sometimes she needed a place where she could forget about schoolwork altogether.

Capoeira provided her with that. She was surrounded by good people, including her best friend Camaleão. Her self-esteem improved with each class as she became more proficient as a capoeirista. There were times when she would arrive early at the academy stressed out about her schoolwork. We talked and I would share with her similar experiences from my life that I thought might be helpful. Her father was not in her life, so I became a male figure that she could talk to. Afterwards, we would have capoeira class and she would work hard. By the end of the night, the stress that she carried coming into class would be gone or diminished.

Panteira worked hard all through high school, taking advanced placement courses, maintaining a 4.0 GPA, working a job part-time on the weekends, and training capoeira. Her diligence and work ethic paid off. She was accepted to several of the top universities in the country, including one that offered her a full scholarship. Her future is infinitely bright, and as she said in her college applications, capoeira played a crucial role in preparing her for college and life.

**Cabelo** is the quintessential old soul. The first incident that comes to mind when I think of Cabelo took place on a Saturday afternoon. I had taught capoeira class that morning, and afterwards Cabelo, Pintado, and Macaco (or as I liked to call them, *Doido* 1, *Doido* 2, and *Doido* 3) came over to the house to help me make *berimbaus*. While we were on my back patio shaving the bark off the wood we planned to utilize for the *berimbaus*, Cabelo asked me if I would teach him how to drive. His father had abandoned him and his family a while back, and he needed someone to step into that role.

I thought back to when I was sixteen—I couldn't wait to learn how to drive so I could go out with my friends. I jokingly asked Cabelo, "You want me to teach you how to drive so you can take a girl out on a date?" He quickly and seriously replied, "No. I want to learn so I can drive my mom to work. She has to catch the bus and I don't like that." I was blown away, but if you were to know Cabelo, then you would know this is just how he is.

When he started training capoeira with me, Cabelo was on the fence between the right path and wrong path. By his nature he was always a good kid, but the prevalence of negativity in the neighborhood was starting to overwhelm him. There was a short while when he was considering making a bad choice. Fortunately, he lived on the same block as Pintado, and Pintado brought him to capoeira class. Cabelo took to it like a fish to water. Cabelo was a thinker, so he naturally had the strategic mind of a capoeirista. This allowed him to excel at the game. So for the couple of years when he was vulnerable to the negative forces in his community, capoeira was able to stabilize his life.

Cabelo

After about five years of training capoeira, Cabelo all but quit training during his junior year of high school. He was the oldest of four kids, and with age he came to recognize the financial stress that his mother was under trying to provide for their family. He started working almost full-time in the afternoons, nights, and on weekends, while staying in school and keeping his grades up.

I was sad not to have Cabelo around at class every day because of the amazing energy that he brought with him, but I was extremely proud to see him step up and care for his family in that way. Cabelo bought himself and his mom each a car so that no one had to take the bus anymore, and he helped pay the bills. No one forced him to do this. One morning, as a sixteen-year-old young man, he recognized a need and decided to do something about it even though it required a large amount of self-sacrifice. After high school he went on to college. He still drops by class sometimes to train or play a few games in the *roda* and to update me on the family.

**Pente** was/is one of the most dedicated students I have ever had. He has never been concerned with status, ego, and fame. When he first started capoeira, all he wanted was to train. His natural abilities were evident from day one, but his work ethic, together with his humility, allowed him to reach a high level of proficiency. It was as if he had been looking for his calling, and when he encountered capoeira he found it.

Pente comes from west Oakland and a working-class family. He's the middle of five children, and as a result he became adept at blending into the background. His being from west Oakland comprised a huge part of his identity, almost defining him completely. His family lived there, he went to school there, all of his friends were from "the west," and he spent almost all his time there. This proved to be somewhat problematic because for all of the good that is in west Oakland—and there is plenty of good there—it is a section of town plagued by drugs and violence. The trappings of Pente's neighborhood surrounded him every day and only increased in intensity as he aged. By the time he was in his late teens—Pente began training with me when he was sixteen—many of his closest friends and others surrounding him were involved in illegal activities. This frightened me to no end because I knew Pente's reality quite well; I had lived it as a teenager myself. The saving grace for me was that I moved out of my neighborhood one week after my high school graduation, allowing me the room to grow into the man I wanted to become.

Recognizing Pente's intense desire to train capoeira, I kept him close to me, training almost every day. Eventually he ended up living with me. I couldn't take him out of Oakland to live since I lived in Oakland, but I could give him a place to go outside west Oakland.

It was a good move. Pente had dropped out of high school, but after beginning his training with me, he returned to school and earned his high school diploma. After several years of training capoeira, Pente accompanied me to Brazil in 2001 to participate in the Copa das Americas. At that time he was a yellow/orange cord, which in our school represents an intermediate-level student, and at this event Pente won the gold medal for his level!

Pente continued to progress as a capoeirista, and in 2004 at the first Capoeira Games of North America, Pente won the overall gold medal for the advanced-level competition.

Pente immersed himself in capoeira, using what it offered to improve his life, eventually enrolling in community college. Through capoeira he has traveled to Brazil, New York, and LA, teaching and playing capoeira with others from all over the world. More importantly, he didn't become a sad statistic like many of the young men from his neighborhood.

I sacrificed a lot of myself to establish my capoeira class, but knowing that my sacrifice helped produce inspiring stories like these reminds me that the effort wasn't in vain. My heart is happy and my soul is rich knowing that there are so many lives I had the ability to affect in a positive way. We came a long way together from the self-made *berimbau* and the crappy *pandeiro* that I started with. After ten years of diligent effort, a lot more people are able to live freer and happier lives, and I thank God and my ancestors for allowing me to be a part of it.

# Conclusion

I often try to visualize what the *rodas* were like three hundred years ago. I imagine how those capoeiristas' voices sounded as they sang their *ladainhas* with heavy hearts, and what those same voices sounded like when the energy of the *roda* had carried them far away from their oppressive reality, allowing them to feel free. I imagine Mestre Bimba as a young capoeirista who worked on the docks all day, and then found time to play and teach capoeira. I recall the stories my mestre has told me about what it was like when he first started capoeira, and of the *rodas* he participated in over the years. When I think of these things, I also think about how I, along with scores of other non-Brazilian capoeiristas, have become a part of the rich tradition and history of capoeira.

Capoeira is symbolized by the *roda*. When a *roda* is established, those people are forming a world of their own. They are a self-contained community. The notion of community can't be separated from capoeira, and as the art form has grown—from the plantations to the cities and *favelas,* throughout Brazil, and finally beyond its borders to encompass the globe—so has the community of capoeira. Capoeiristas are Brazilian, but they are also Japanese, Italian, Senegalese, Canadian, French, etc. Capoeiristas now have multiple countries of origin.

One of the remarkable aspects of my group in California is its international composition. I have students from the United States,

Laos, Mexico, El Salvador, Poland, China, Nigeria, Puerto Rico, Vietnam, and Bosnia. Regardless of their country of origin, the philosophies of capoeira were readily received by these individuals and blended into the greater world view given them by their respective cultures. A Nigerian Muslim woman can be a capoeirista. A Mexican Catholic man is also a capoeirista. And as capoeira has gone international, affecting the lives of so many diverse practitioners, these capoeiristas have brought their diversity with them, impacting the greater capoeira community.

When I wrote about the oppressive forces within capoeira, I wrote about them from my world view as an African-American man. This world view may agree with that of many other cultures, and there may be many other world views that are at odds with it. Nonetheless, the African-American world view, along with the host of other cultures previously referenced, is becoming integrated into the global capoeira community. Brazil is home to capoeira, but capoeira now lives outside Brazil as well.

The young people I taught committed themselves to the game. Their dedication isn't surpassed by anyone's. They play all the *toques* of the *berimbau* with precision, their capoeira is as rich as that of their Brazilian counterparts, and they know the history and philosophy of capoeira. Yet they didn't learn capoeira in Salvador, or Rio, or Recife. These youngsters learned capoeira in east Oakland. This is the beauty of the light of capoeira spreading throughout the world. From a slave tradition in Brazil, capoeira has grown to teach people around the world how to walk through life.

# Glossary

**Agogô:** Cowbell used as part of the *bateria,* or orchestra/band in a capoeira circle.

**Angola:** *Berimbau* rhythm calling for Capoeira Angola to be played.

**Armada:** Spinning circular kick.

**Armada Dupla:** Leaping acrobatic movement executing *armada* with both legs simultaneously.

**Atabaque:** Drum used as part of the *bateria.*

**Bateria:** Collective arrangement of capoeira instruments.

**Batizado:** Graduation ceremony in which new students are initiated into the capoeira community by playing with a mestre; additionally used to promote students through the various cord levels.

**Benguela:** *Berimbau* rhythm calling for a *Benguela* game to be played; this game emphasizes cunning, grace, and fluidity and is played at a medium tempo.

**Berimbau:** Bowed string instrument of capoeira; leader of the *bateria.*

**Besouro Preto:** Mythical figure in the history of capoeira who is believed to have been an expert capoeirista with magical powers who defended the poor and weak.

**Boca de Espera:** A stalking, waiting game of capoeira; considered to be bad form.

**Cabeçada:** A movement using your head to strike your opponent.

**Capoeira:** Art form invented by enslaved Africans combining martial arts, dance, music, and tradition; the word also referred to areas of short brush in Brazil, believed to have concealed the training of capoeiristas.

**Capoeira Angola:** Traditional capoeira pre-dating Capoeira Regional.

**Capoeira Regional:** The more regimented martial arts-oriented capoeira style developed by Mestre Bimba.

**Capoeirista:** Practitioner of capoeira.

**Favela:** Slum; poor neighborhood.

**Gancho:** Snapping heel kick.

**Ginga:** Swinging rhythmic motion of capoeira, said to mimic the swaying of the ocean.

**Gunga:** The deepest-pitched *berimbau*.

**Iúna:** Capoeira rhythm calling for an *Iúna* game to be played; intended for graduated students and above, this game emphasizes acrobatics and shows of strength, balance, and grace.

**Jogo Bonito:** "The beautiful game," referring to capoeira.

**Ladainha:** Traditional song ("litany") in capoeira that tells a story; normally sung to begin a *roda* in which Capoeira Angola will be played.

**Ladrão:** Criminal.

**Luta Regional Baiana:** Original name of Mestre Bimba's methodological approach to teaching and playing capoeira; later called Capoeira Regional.

**Ma'afa:** The great tragedy known as the trans-Atlantic slave trade.

**Malícia:** An alert mental state cautious of danger.

**Mandinga:** The ability to manipulate the game and your opponent to your liking.

**Mandinguero:** Someone who plays with *mandinga*.

**Martelo:** hammer kick

**Medio:** Medium-pitched *berimbau*.

**Meia-Lua-de-Compasso:** Spinning heel kick imitating the arc traced by a compass drawing a circle.

**Pandeiro:** Tambourine used as part of the *bateria*.

**Pé do Berimbau:** Meaning "foot of the berimbau," this is the spot in the *roda* beneath the *berimbau(s)* where capoeiristas begin their games.

**Queda de Rins:** Balancing movement in which the entire body's weight is leveraged on the elbow.

**Rasteira:** Sweep used to take down an opponent.

**Reco-Reco:** Ridged instrument that forms part of the *bateria*.

**Roda:** Circle in which capoeira is played.

**Rolê:** Rolling movement used by capoeiristas to travel in the *roda*.

**Tesoura:** scissors take-down